John Webster

Twayne's English Authors Series

Arthur F. Kinney, Editor

University of Massachusetts, Amherst

TEAS 465

Portrait of King James I and his Family, Living and Dead, with Verses Attributed to John Webster. Copy of the 1633 issue of an engraving dated 1624–25.

Reproduced courtesy of the Trustees of the British Museum, London.

John Webster

Margaret Loftus Ranald

Queens College of the City University of New York

Twayne Publishers
A Division of G.K. Hall & Co. • *Boston*

John Webster

Margaret Loftus Ranald

Copyright © 1989 by G. K. Hall & Co.
All Rights Reserved.
Published by Twayne Publishers
A Division of G. K. Hall & Co.
70 Lincoln Street
Boston, Massachusetts 02111

Copyediting supervised by Barbara Sutton
Book Production by Patricia D'Agostino
Book Design by Barbara Anderson

Typeset in 11 pt. Garamond
by Williams Press Inc.

Printed on permanent/durable acid-free paper
and bound in the United States of America

Library of Congress Cataloging-in-Publication Data

Ranald, Margaret Loftus.
    John Webster / Margaret Loftus Ranald.
        p.   cm.—(Twayne's English authors series ; TEAS 465)
    Bibliography: p.
    Includes index.
    ISBN 0-8057-6976-5 (alk. paper)
    1. Webster, John, 1580?–1625?—Criticism and interpretation.
I. Title. II. Series.
PR3187R3   1989
822'.3—dc19

                                                                88–31273
                                                                CIP

For Ralph and Caroline
as always

Contents

Editor's Note

The dark tragedies of John Webster speak powerfully to our own times, as Margaret Loftus Ranald makes clear in this compact but remarkably comprehensive study of his life and works. The successor to William Shakespeare as the chief dramatist for the King's Men, Webster in his passionate "night-pieces" gave to the English Renaissance stage its most fully developed and most memorable roles for women, searing psychological portraits in which his unsparing view of the random fate to which the human condition is subjected remains one of the period's most memorable achievements. Ranald's study shows how Webster's sense of decay and corruption in the world around him was the source of a tragic view of man's existence, its sense of fragility, amorality, and despair a central part of man's experience. By refusing to ignore the horrors of his tragic imagination, Webster pursued a vision of man's fate that is as potent now as it was when it was first presented before Jacobean audiences.

This study of John Webster's life and works examines all that is known of his life and analyzes all of his work that is now extant—his two major tragedies, *The White Devil* and *The Duchess of Malfi;* his undeservedly neglected tragicomedy, *The Devil's Law-Case;* his authentic collaborations; and his Overburian characters and occasional poetry. Ranald has also supplied an exceptionally thorough bibliography of primary sources and a selected, annotated bibliography of secondary works to aid readers and students in further study.

Arthur F. Kinney

About the Author

Margaret Loftus Ranald received her B.A. in French and English, her M.A. with honors in English from Victoria University of Wellington, New Zealand. After receiving a Fulbright Travel Grant she earned her M.A. and Ph.D. from the University of California, Los Angeles. She has taught at Temple University, and is now professor of English at Queens College of the City University of New York. She has also been visiting professor at UCLA.

The author of numerous articles, papers, and reviews on Shakespeare, Shelley, Joyce, and other writers, Professor Ranald's specialty is the study of drama, both as literary and performance art. She is the author of *The Eugene O'Neill Companion* (Westport, Conn.: Greenwood Press, 1984) and *Shakespeare and His Social Context: Studies in Osmotic Knowledge and Literary Interpretation* (New York: AMS Press, 1987).

Preface

This book is intended to be an introduction to the work of John Webster, whose two great tragedies, *The White Devil* and *The Duchess of Malfi,* are frequently ranked second only to the work of Shakespeare in the history of British drama.

In recent years Webster scholarship has undergone a renaissance and a number of important book-length studies have appeared, particularly *John Webster: A Reference Guide,* by Samuel Schuman (Boston: G.K. Hall, 1985), covering scholarship through 1981, and the monumental work by Charles R. Forker, *Skull Beneath the Skin: The Achievement of John Webster* (Carbondale and Edwardsville: Southern Illinois University Press, 1986). With such scholarly materials available, this introductory study aims to present as much basic information as possible within its limited compass, including studies of texts, sources, authorship, and plot synopses. Guidance is offered through critical comment. The bibliography is also deliberately restricted to accounts of the primary works, editions, bibliographies, and a highly selected group of secondary sources. The user is given guidelines for further research in, and additional reading about, this astonishingly unexpected playwright, whose identity has but recently been convincingly established.

John Webster spent the greater part of his creative life as a collaborator with other, and more famous, playwrights on a series of journeyman dramas. Then suddenly he stepped forth from the shadows with a small, but extremely distinguished corpus of independent work, a mere three plays of which *The White Devil* and *The Duchess of Malfi* are preeminent Jacobean tragedies, while *The Devil's Law-Case* is a quintessentially complex tragicomedy. What differentiates these works from the rest of Elizabethan and Jacobean drama is their unique skepticism, their unflinching acceptance of the fate of humankind in a world in which old beliefs were being challenged and new ones had not yet been found to fill the void.

Also surprising is Webster's modernity, particularly in his treatment of feminine characters. He is not afraid to portray women of power, whether evil (yet strangely admirable) like Vittoria Corombona in *The White Devil,* dignified and tragic, like the Duchess of Malfi, or manipulative, like Leonora in *The Devil's Law-Case*. What these three have in common is independence and strength of will, a commitment to a course of action which they have freely chosen without care for the consequences. In other words, they choose to take risks and in so doing they broaden the female horizons of the Jacobean era, while at the same time undermining norms of established behavior.

The major emphasis of this book is on the three great independent plays and their unique contribution to English dramatic literature. However, there is also extended discussion of the collaborations, insofar as Webster's individual hand can be determined. In addition, his nondramatic work as a character writer, social critic, and writer of occasional verse is also noted, for frequently it contains the germ of a dramatic portrait or event. Webster is at times lethal in his portraits of rogues, and lyrical in his celebration of virtue. Overall, the playwright has given a remarkably broad and detailed account of London life, while at the same time portraying the evil that lurks in the hearts of humanity. His villains and wicked brothers remain unforgettable and he does not take the easy way out when his heroines confront the consequences of their independence. He maintains an unusual degree of intellectual flexibility, of sympathetic objectivity even toward his evil characters, because for him they remain human beings.

The organization is basically chronological, except for treatment of the nondramatic works, because the playwright arranged his productive life in an unusually symmetrical manner, both beginning and ending his career working anonymously, and chameleonlike, with other playwrights. From all these experiences, and from the voluminous reading he enshrined in his notebooks, Webster learned the art of transmutation. The bare bones of fact and the words of others are touched by his philosopher's stone of poetic composition to become economical statements of surpassing pathos and the purest of gold.

The editions of Webster's work cited in the text are as follows:

For the minor works, nondramatic items, and collaborations I have used *The Complete Works of John Webster,* ed. F.L. Lucas, 4 vols. (London: Chatto & Windus, 1927–28). Where Lucas omits material, such as Webster's collaborations with Thomas Dekker on *Westward Ho!* and *Northward Ho!*, I have used *The Dramatic Works of Thomas Dekker,* ed. Fredson Bowers, 4 vols. (Cambridge: Cambridge University Press, 1953–61). Similarly, where the Lucas texts of the major plays have been superseded, I have chosen others.

For *The While Devil* and *The Duchess of Malfi* I have used the Revels Edition, ed. John Russell Brown (London: Methuen, 1960 and 1964), and for *The Devil's Law-Case* the Regents Renaissance Edition, ed. Frances A. Shirley (Lincoln: University of Nebraska Press, 1972). These, it should be noted, are the same as those used by Forker (1986), a choice meant to facilitate the work of a researcher.

Margaret Loftus Ranald

Queens College of the City University of New York

Acknowledgments

With gratitude I acknowledge the assistance of Arthur F. Kinney of the University of Massachusetts, Amherst; Lewis De Simone, my editor at Twayne; and the staffs at the Folger Shakespeare Library, the Henry E. Huntington Library and Art Gallery, and the Library of Queens College, the City University of New York. For help in obtaining texts I thank Charles Forker of Indiana University, William Green of Queens College, and especially my former chair, Robert Hamilton Ball, Professor Emeritus at Queens College, for the thoughtful gift of his personal Webster collection, which made my work so much easier.

The Trustees of the British Museum granted permission to reproduce as frontispiece the unique 1633 issue of a 1624–25 engraving of King James I and his family, with verses by John Webster, transcribed in the Appendix.

I also extend thanks to the City University of New York and Queens College for the award of a Faculty Development Grant to learn word processing and to the patience of Dragonfly Software in explaining arcane aspects of *Nota Bene*. Lastly, I thank my companionable paperweights, Demelza and Roxelana (cats), and above all my husband, Ralph, for his extraordinary patience, encouragement—and love.

Chronology

1579–1580   The playwright John Webster born in London to John Webster, Sr., a member of the Merchant Taylors' Company, and Elizabeth Coates Webster.

1588?   ? John Webster enters the Merchant Taylors' School.

1598   1 August: John Webster, probably the playwright, is admitted to the Middle Temple from New Inn.

1602   May–June: A play named *Two Shapes* is commissioned by Philip Henslowe; collaborators are Thomas Dekker, Michael Drayton, Thomas Middleton, Anthony Munday, and John Webster. 22 May: A play named *Caesar's Fall* is accepted by Philip Henslowe, with payment of £5 to the Admiral's Men, Anthony Munday, Thomas Middleton, Michael Drayton, "Webster & the Rest." Probably the same play as *Two Shapes*. 15 and 21 October: Philip Henslowe makes payments for a play named *Lady Jane* to Henry Chettle, Thomas Dekker, Wentworth Smith, and John Webster. 2, 23, 26 November: Philip Henslowe makes payments to Henry Chettle, Thomas Dekker, and John Webster for *Christmas Comes but Once a Year* (lost). Writes verses prefacing part 3 of Anthony Munday's *Palmerin of England*.

1604   Collaborates with Thomas Dekker on *Westward Ho!* for the Children of Paul's. Writes an introductory ode for Stephen Harrison's *Arches of Triumph*. Writes the *Induction* to John Marston's *The Malcontent* for a performance by the King's Men.

1605   18 March: Marries Sara, daughter of Simon Peniall, warden of the Saddlers' Company. Collaborates with Thomas Dekker on *Northward Ho!* for the Children of Paul's.

1606   8 May: John, son of John Webster, is baptized at St. Dunstan's in the West.

1607   *Sir Thomas Wyatt* (probably incorporating the 1602 *Lady Jane*) published. *Westward Ho!* and *Northward Ho!* published.

1610–1619 Writes *The Devil's Law-Case* (date of composition disputed).

1612 3 February: Edward Webster, playwright's brother, admitted to the Merchant Taylors' Company after completing his apprenticeship. 10 February: Edward Webster marries Margaret Allen at the church of St. Peter-le-Poor. *The White Devil* published. Performed by the Red Bull Company, probably early in the year. Writes commendatory verses to *An Apology for Actors* by Thomas Heywood.

1613 Contributes a poem to *A Monumental Column,* a series of poems on the death of Prince Henry, entered in the *Stationers' Register,* 26 December 1613–14. *The Duchess of Malfi* acted at the Blackfriars Theatre by the King's Men.

1614–1615 John Webster, Sr., dies. ? *The Guise* (lost), acted.

1615 June: Admitted to membership in the Merchant Taylors' by right of primogeniture as one "borne free" of the company. Edits the sixth edition of Thomas Overbury's *Characters,* contributing "An Excellent Actor," among thirty-two additional characters.

1617–1620 *The Devil's Law-Case* performed by Queen Anne's Men, probably at the Cockpit.

1617 Webster is satirized by Henry Fitzjeffrey, of Lincoln's Inn.

1621 2 October: Edward Webster marries Susan Walker Llewellyn, widow. ? *Anything for a Quiet Life* written by Thomas Middleton, probably with John Webster. Date and authorship both disputed; cannot be later than 1627, when Middleton died.

1623 *The Duchess of Malfi* published. *The Devil's Law-Case* published with a dedication mentioning the lost play *The Guise.* Writes verses prefixed to Henry Cockeram's *The English Dictionarie.* . . .

1624 3–15 September: *A Late Murther of the Son upon the Mother, or Keep the Widow Waking* (lost) written by Thomas Dekker, John Ford, William Rowley, and John Webster, licensed for performance at the Red Bull. 29 October: *Monuments of Honor,* a pageant prepared by the Merchant

Taylors' Company for the inauguration of John Gore, Merchant Taylor, as Lord Mayor of London, performed and published 1624–25. ? Verses on an Engraving of King James I and His Family, Living and Dead (after September 1624).

1624–1625 ? *A Cure for a Cuckold,* by John Webster ? and William Rowley.

1625–1626 22 January: *The Fair Maid of the Inn,* by John Webster ? John Fletcher, John Ford, and Philip Massinger, licensed for performance by the King's Men at Blackfriars.

1626–1627 ? *Appius and Virginia,* with Thomas Heywood, may have been written as late as this date. No further records of Webster. May have died any time after 1628, although 1632–34 seems the most likely period.

1635 Oblique reference to Webster in *The Hierarchie of the Blessed Angels* by Thomas Heywood.

1647 *The Fair Maid of the Inn* published as part of the folio edition of the works of Francis Beaumont and John Fletcher, where it is assigned to Fletcher.

1654 *Appius and Virginia* published.

1661 *A Cure for a Cuckold* published.

1662 *Anything for a Quiet Life* published.

Chapter One
Life and Background

Family

Of all the Elizabethan and Jacobean dramatists, John Webster remains the most shadowy. Indeed, until 1976, when Mary Edmond began publishing the results of her research, the basic facts of his identity were unknown.[1] Even now, when something definite is known of his family, many unanswered questions remain. For instance, specific details concerning his birth, education, and the beginning of his connection with the theater are still based on supposition. But at least his social and geographical milieu is no longer a mystery.

The playwright John Webster was the son of John Webster, carriage maker, who resided in the parish of St. Sepulchre-without-Newgate, and whose business was located at the corner of Hosier and Cow lanes in Smithfield, an unfashionable part of London, close to Newgate Prison and the Central Criminal Court. Since Websters seem to have lived for some time in the parish, the playwright's father, John Webster, Sr., may well have been London-born. In 1571, probably after the customary seven-year apprenticeship, he was made free of the Merchant Taylors' Company; he then must have been about the age of twenty-one. These figures indicate a birthdate of 1550 or a little earlier. Freedom of a guild company gave a young man the right to set himself up in business and to marry. On 4 November 1577 John Webster, Sr., married Elizabeth Coates of the parish of St. Giles, Cripplegate, whose father was a blacksmith. A union between two allied trades such as coachmaking and blacksmithing would obviously be an economic advantage.

Unfortunately, since the records of St. Sepulchre's parish were destroyed in the Great Fire of London in 1666, it is impossible to date accurately the births of his sons John and Edward. John, however, is presumed to have been the elder for two reasons: first, he was named for his father, and second, he himself was admitted to the Merchant Taylors' Company in June 1615, by right of birth, after the death of his father. This is what the playwright meant when he later identified himself as

1

"one borne free" of the Merchant Taylors'. Edward, on the other hand, had been admitted earlier, on 3 February 1611/12, after serving his time as an apprentice.[2] The playwright thus would seem to have been born around 1579, with Edward born some few years later.[3]

At first glance the connection between John Webster, coachmaker, and the Merchant Taylors' Company appears strange, but the trade of coachmaker was so new that a separate guild did not exist until 1677; Therefore in Webster's time a man of his craft needed the umbrella of an existing organization. Cooperation with the Merchant Taylors' Company was quite logical because that guild was responsible for making the funeral trappings of hearses, the hangings for plays and pageants, and even the curtained booth stages for traveling companies, all of which were either displayed on or transported by the vehicles produced by the coachmakers. In addition, the development of coaches as a luxurious mode of transportation generated additional employment for upholsterers and allied trades within the Merchant Taylors'.

John Webster, Sr., would have supplied rental coaches and carts for other purposes as well, including punishment. Petty criminals were often "carted" through town, tied to the tail of a cart and whipped, while criminals guilty of major offenses like treason were taken by wagon to the execution site at Tyburn. Hence these vehicles were sometimes called "Tyburn carts." With a father in this line of business, perhaps the playwright's interest in death is not surprising. But even more likely, his gloomy preoccupation was strengthened by the plague years during which the dead were merely left outside their houses to be picked up by collectors of corpses in *their* carts—presumably supplied by such businessmen as John Webster, Sr.

Another continual reminder of the proximity of death was provided by one Robert Dowe (or Dove), who in 1605 gave £50 to Webster's parish church of St. Sepulchre for the clerk to toll the great bell of the church the evening before an execution at Tyburn. In addition, the clerk was to go at midnight to the cell of the condemned man in Newgate with a handbell and ring twelve strokes upon it, all the time exhorting the criminal to repent.[4] Webster's father was one of the twenty-four leading parishioners and four common councilmen of the church who signed the document relating to this charitable foundation. One further connection with the Webster family is that Dowe was himself a member of the Merchant Taylors' Company.[5] This bequest financed the office of "the common bell-man"—later mentioned by Bosola in *The Duchess of Malfi*.

The playwright's father became a very prosperous businessman, as his offices in his church prove, and one should not be misled into surmising that Webster's origins were lower class, even though his place of residence might seem to indicate this. Convenience and common sense dictated placing the coach manufacturing business adjacent to the Smithfield horse market, and its other allied trades such as harnessmaking and saddlery. In addition, the area just outside the City Wall offered sufficient space for the display of coaches, charrettes, and carts. Such was the growth of the coach industry that by the end of the sixteenth century complaints about traffic congestion on the narrow, winding streets of London were already frequent. Others objected that coaches contributed to immorality by making possible the private transportation of participants either actively engaged in, or being taken to illicit assignations.

Education

Certainly, since John Webster, *père*, was a fairly senior member in good standing in his guild, one would expect that his son should attend the prestigious Merchant Taylors' School, which had reached illustrious heights under the guidance of its first headmaster, William Mulcaster, author of two important pedagogical tracts, the *Elementarie* (1582) and *Positions* (1581), and one of the most influential educators of his day. This school was designed primarily for secular rather than religious education. The plan of studies was heavily classical, but Mulcaster in particular was one of those enlightened people who was proud of his native tongue. In the *Elementarie* he emphasizes the importance of clear writing in English; after paying homage to the classics he proclaims the justly famous line, "I honor the Latin, but I worship the *English*."[6]

Unfortunately, no documents survive to prove that John Webster ever attended the Merchant Taylors' School; other evidence of his having acquired any solid classical and linguistic training is also sadly lacking. Throughout his writing career he habitually used a translation if one existed, rather than referring to the original text. If, however, he did indeed attend the Merchant Taylors' School, he would have entered around 1588, at about the age of nine, and would have remained there until he was fifteen or sixteen. An important part of the curriculum, because the boys of the Merchant Taylors' School were accustomed to taking part in the various kinds of pageants and ceremonies of the city, was the performance of plays, both classical and vernacular, as a means of inculcating ease of manner and developing elocutionary facility. John

Webster, Sr., also had some connection with these city celebrations; in 1602, for instance, he was paid 30 shillings by the Merchant Taylors' for the hire of horses and carts to transport the boys of their school on the day of the pageant inaugurating Sir Henry Lee, a Merchant Taylor, as Lord Mayor.[7]

Webster and the Law

At this point two self-canceling theories arise concerning the life of John Webster. The first possibility (admittedly rather unlikely) concerns a John Wobster [sic], who in the year 1596 appears in Cassel, Germany, with one Robert Browne as part of a touring English theatrical group that had been acting in Germany since the early 1590s. "Wobster" could well be a misprint for "Webster," who would at this time probably have been sixteen to eighteen. If this is the playwright, presumably apprenticed earlier as a child actor, one must reluctantly abandon the possibility of his having spent much time, if any, at the Merchant Taylors' School. But however tempting it may be to think that John Webster had some early personal professional connection with the theater, certain identification is impossible. One thing is sure: Webster's father had some connection with theatrical persons quite early, because in 1591 John and Edward Alleyn owed him some 15 shillings for an unspecified reason.[8]

The second possibility concerns the record of a John Webster who on 1 August 1598 was admitted to the Middle Temple from New Inn. Clearly, John Wobster the actor and John Webster the student at the Middle Temple cannot be the same person, because the actor could not have had sufficient education to qualify for admission. Therefore, the identification of the playwright with a graduate of the Merchant Taylors' School and prospective lawyer seems more likely. A student going to one of the Inns of Court (the others being Gray's and Lincoln's Inns) would usually enter at the age of sixteen or seventeen and after two years of preparatory training would proceed to the corresponding senior institution, in this case the Middle Temple. In effect, these institutions formed a kind of university within the city and frequently their students had already spent some time at one of the two universities of Oxford and Cambridge.[9] Both the Inns of Chancery and the Temple were noted for their interest in literature and theatrical performances; professional companies (including Shakespeare's) played in their great halls and their grand Christmas entertainments were justly famous. If

Webster was indeed a student there his interest in theater would surely have been stimulated further, perhaps by actual participation as writer or actor.

At this time attempts were being made to restrict the legal profession to those of gentle birth, something Webster quite clearly was not. In practice, however, the sons of tradesmen of sufficient wealth and successful entrepreneurial skills were considered eligible. The designation of the entrant at the Middle Temple as the son of John Webster, gentleman (the Latin text uses the term *generosus*), may thus be a legal fiction to justify the future playwright's admission.[10] Certainly, whoever this John Webster was, he did not complete the seven-year course (including time at an Inn of Chancery), because he was never called to the bar.

If Webster did study at the Middle Temple, he would also have obtained firsthand experience of the dramatic possibilities inherent in public legal confrontations, since a considerable portion of the curriculum then (as now) consisted of moot courts and discussions of important legal cases. Further, Webster's evident knowledge of the law and its ramifications, together with his notable animus against dishonest lawyers, well demonstrated in *The Devil's Law-Case* and his lethal characterizations of *A Puny-clarke* and *A meere Petifogger,* appear to indicate intimate relationship with, and study of the discipline. Similarly, he also shows fervent appreciation of an honest legal expert in the character of *A Reverend Judge.* But what continues to give pause in this matter of legal education is the playwright's known deficiency in classical learning, which makes one wonder whether he was in truth a fitting candidate for the Temple.

Early Career as Dramatist

Webster then disappears from recorded fact until 1602/3, when he appears as a collaborator on three dramas, the lost play *Caesar's Fall* (probably the same as *Two Shapes,* also lost), *Lady Jane* (probably surviving in the printed version of *Sir Thomas Wyatt*), and *Christmas Comes but Once a Year* (lost, but presumably a seasonal potboiler). The established dramatists with whom he was associated at the time were generally much better known than he, including Henry Chettle, Thomas Dekker, Michael Drayton, Thomas Middleton, Anthony Munday, and the now forgotten Wentworth Smith. At the close of his first year of collaboration, Webster also wrote some introductory verses to the romance

The Palmerin of England, which had been written by his collaborator Anthony Munday.

What brought Webster into this literary milieu is not clear, but from this time he was a busy writer, possibly through his connection with Thomas Dekker. In 1604 he collaborated with Dekker on a citizen comedy, *Westward Ho!,* for the Children of Paul's, and with John Marston on the *Induction* to and revisions of Marston's earlier play *The Malcontent,* then being performed by the King's Men, the adult company at the Globe Theatre whose primary dramatist was Shakespeare. It is just possible that Webster and Marston had become acquainted while they were both at the Middle Temple. Acquaintance with Dekker may also be the reason that Webster was invited to contribute an introductory ode to *Arches of Triumph* (1604), the opulent published volume commemorating the belated pageantry welcoming King James I to London in 1604. The collaboration of the two authors continued, and in 1605 they produced a second merry and bawdy citizen comedy, *Northward Ho!,* in response to *Eastward Ho!,* the work of a rival consortium from the Children of the Queen's Revels, which had in turn been devised as a reply to the earlier *Westward Ho!*

Marriage and Later Life

On 18 March 1605/6 Webster married Sara Peniall, daughter of the warden of the Saddlers' Company and a parishioner of St. Dunstan's in the West. Once again in the Webster family a marriage took place between allied trades. This ceremony, however, took place not in the bride's parish but in St. Mary's, Islington, during Lent, usually a forbidden season for marriages. However, less than two months after the wedding their first child (also named John) was baptized at St. Dunstan's in the West, on 8 May; thus haste, a special dispensation, and privacy were essential.[11] Apparently other children were born, though their ages are unknown, because two bequests name Margery, Sara, Elizabeth, John, and "the rest of Websters children."[12] That this is the right family seems certain since three of these names can be traced back to the dramatist's forebears.

From this time on, documentation of John Webster's life, apart from information on the publication and performance of his plays, is astonishingly sparse. On 3 February 1611/12, his younger brother Edward was admitted to the Merchant Taylors' Company after serving his apprenticeship. Presumably he married almost immediately, for a record documents the marriage of an Edward Webster to a Margaret Allen at the Church of St. Peter-le-Poor, near Merchant Taylors' Hall, one week later. Apparently (if this is the right Edward Webster), Margaret died, because on 2 October 1621 Edward married a widow, Susan Llewellyn, by license in New Brentford. She was the daughter of John Walker, Gentleman, a local resident in Green Dragon Court, off Cow Lane. On 8 April 1614 John Webster, Sr., made his will and seems to have died sometime between that date and 19 June 1615,[13] when his son John, the playwright, presented himself for membership in the Merchant Taylors' by right of birth as an eldest son under the sponsorship of two other members of the company, neither of them his relations.[14]

Reputation and Compositional Practice

By this time John Webster had achieved some fame, both as collaborator and independent dramatist, having published *The White Devil* in 1612, the year of its first performance. The following year *The Duchess of Malfi* received its first performance, with publication in 1623. Some time between 1617 and 1620 *The Devil's Law-Case* was written and performed, and in 1618 a strange satire appeared with a reference to Webster, which for many years defied interpretation.[15] This was a collection entitled *Certain Elegies Done by Sundrie Excellent Wits*, one section of which, written by Henry Fitzjeffrey, was "Intituled *Notes from Black Fryers*,," and included the now well-known attack on John Webster as "Crabbed (*Websterio*) / The *Play-wright, Cart-wright*". The poem criticizes Webster for his notorious slowness and difficulty in composition.

> Was euer man so mangl'd with a *Poem?*
> See how he drawes his mouth awry of late,
> How he scrubs: wrings his wrests: scratches his Pate
> A *Midwife!* helpe By his *Braines coitus,*
> Some *Centaure* strange: Some huge *Bucephalus,*
> Or *Pallas* (sure) ingendred in his *Braine,*
> Strike *Vulcan* with thy hammer once againe.[16]

Now, with the identification of Webster's family, the reference to a cart is obvious, and since the playwright himself remarked that he did not *"write with a goose-quill, winged with two feathers,"*[17] it is clear that Webster's laborious industry was famous, and that he himself was well aware of his problem.

An even more important, if highly curious, aspect of Webster's composition is his habit of continually borrowing from others without attribution. More than any other major Elizabethan or Jacobean writer, Webster pillaged and transmuted the work of others, fashioning his appropriations into something apposite and almost entirely new. Like many another person of his time, he doubtless kept what Sir Philip Sidney called "Nizolian paper books," commonplace books in which he jotted down interesting comments, "arresting conceits, pithy sententiae, and striking epigrams."[18] To some extent this practice may have slowed his composition, but it may also indicate a certain insecurity, going hand in hand with his known lack of facility in foreign and classical languages.

But Webster's practice was not mere plagiarism, an act that Renaissance writers and readers regarded differently from us today. Then it was indeed true that "imitation is the sincerest form of flattery" and poets deliberately drew attention to their borrowings. No stigma was attached to such appropriation of the work of others, and indeed the writer was praised for his ability to adapt and improve upon his originals. *Imitatio,* to use the Latin word, was a legitimate rhetorical device; readers enjoyed the intellectual exercise it inspired, and writers rejoiced in it. Webster, for instance, quite clearly polished and honed his borrowings with true poetic power so that they become newly cut and faceted gems within the body of his work.[19] He was a most painstaking artist, and his evident care in composition together with his dissatisfaction with the theatrical reception of *The White Devil* indicates a desire, even a preference, for his works to be studied by the judicious *reader* as well as performed before what he believed to be frequently unappreciative auditors. Perhaps he was too much addicted to the striking phrase or the apothegm, but some of his short utterances remain forever imprinted in the mind, in particular the reaction of Ferdinand to the sight of the corpse of his sister, the Duchess of Malfi (4.2.264).

The Last Years

The only other reference to Webster's own life comes in his last major independent work, *Monuments of Honor,* a pageant devised by Webster for the inauguration of Sir John Gore, the fourth member of the Merchant Taylors' Guild in the playwright's lifetime to be elected Lord Mayor of London. In the introduction to the published text, he boasts of his membership in the company, a circumstance that doubtless contributed to his commission. Nothing else is known of Webster's life or compositional habits. The scholar is left only with four more collaborative works: the lost *A Late Murther of the Son upon the Mother, or Keep the Widow Waking,* written with Thomas Dekker, John Ford, and William Rowley in 1624; two disputed plays, *A Cure for a Cuckold* (1624–25), written with William Rowley, and *The Fair Maid of the Inn* (1625–26), written with John Fletcher, John Ford and Philip Massinger; and *Appius and Virginia,* probably Webster's last work, dating as late as 1625–27, written with Thomas Heywood.

John Webster slips out of life with total anonymity, and his death may have taken place any time after 1628. In 1630, when Sir Robert Ducy, another member of the Merchant Taylors' Guild, became Lord Mayor, one might have expected Webster to have some part in the celebrations, but such was not the case. Then in 1635 Thomas Heywood, Webster's old friend and collaborator, published a celebratory work entitled *The Hierarchie of the Blessed Angels* that includes Webster's name, but since the tenses of this poem are imprecise it is impossible to determine whether he was alive or dead at the time Heywood was writing.

Another curious reference to the playwright indicating something of his reputation appears around 1632 when William Heminges (one of the editors of Shakespeare's First Folio of 1623) wrote a mock elegy concerning the loss of a finger by a fellow actor, Thomas Randolph, in a fight with "a Riotous Gentleman." In it he describes the funeral procession that conducted the finger to its abode across the river Styx, where it had been escorted by Art, Invention, and Imitation:

> Ytt had byn drawne and wee In state aproche
> But Websters brother would nott lend a Coach:
> Hee swore that all were hired to Conuey
> The Malfy Dutches sadly on her way.[20]

This reference would seem to imply that Webster was either still alive or had recently died, because the point of the joke would otherwise have been lost. In light of all this evidence Mary Edmond suggests 1632–34 as the most likely time of his death, but as is so often the case with Webster, certainty eludes us.[21]

The possibility of finding any further evidence concerning Webster's death or burial is now most unlikely, but the provision of further facts about this playwright is insignificant compared with his literary achievement: his interesting collaborations, ranging from the tragic to the contemporary and bawdily comic, a handful of important "Characters" and some nondramatic poems, a remarkable pageant, a skillfully contrived and unjustly neglected legal tragicomedy, an almost unsurpassed gallery of intelligent and independent feminine characters, and two darkly innovative tragedies that demand comparison with the work of his near-contemporary, William Shakespeare.

Chapter Two

Early Dramatic Works: Collaborations

The first mention of John Webster as a professional playwright appears in the diary of the Elizabethan and Jacobean theatrical impresario Philip Henslowe. On 22 May 1602 he records a payment of £5 to Anthony Munday, Thomas Middleton, Michael Drayton, John "Webster & the Rest" for a play entitled *Caesar's Fall* to be performed by the Admiral's Men. On 29 May 1602 another disbursement of £3 was made in "fulle payment" for *Two Shapes*, generally believed to be the same play. Nothing further is known of it, although it might have been intended as competition for Shakespeare's *Julius Caesar* (1599).[1]

Sir Thomas Wyatt

Text, date, sources, and authorship. On 15 October 1602 Henslowe made a payment of 50 shillings to John Webster, Thomas Dekker, Thomas Heywood, Wentworth Smith, and Henry Chettle for *Lady Jane*, to be written for the Earl of Worcester's Men. Full payment of £5/10s. was made when the play was completed on 21 October. That it had some notable success is indicated by a further payment of 5 shillings to Dekker to begin work on *Lady Jane*. Either or both parts would seem to be the play *The Overthrow of Rebels* mentioned elsewhere in Henslowe.

In 1607 the quarto text of another play on the same topic as *Lady Jane* was published, the title page of which reads:

THE / FAMOVS / History of Sir Tho- / mas Wyatt. / *With the Coronation of Queen Mary,* / and the coming in of King / Philip. / As it was plaied by the Queens Maiesties / Seruants. / Written by *Thomas Dickers,* / And *Iohn Webster.* / [Ornament] / *LONDON* / *Printed by E[dward]. A[llde]. for Thomas Archer,* and are to be / solde at his shop in the Popes-head Pallace, / nere the Royall Exchange. / 1607.

This text, a pirated edition not licensed for printing in the *Stationers' Register,* is at best a fourthhand account, deriving from a playhouse performance, with an unknown number of alterations by the actors, reconstructors, and printers. Its "ill-deserved second edition" of 1607, from the same printer, is wholly derivative and offers no improvement on the first edition.[2] No act and scene divisions are given in either text. Webster's contributions to the play we now possess are impossible to determine with any accuracy, since "We cannot know how Webster may have written ten years before *The White Devil*";[3] nonetheless, there are foreshadowings of both that play and *The Duchess of Malfi.*

The sources of *Sir Thomas Wyatt* are Raphael Holinshed's *Chronicles,* John Stow's *Annals,* John Foxe's *Acts and Monuments* (popularly known as *Foxe's Book of Martyrs*), and Richard Grafton's *Chronicles.*

Stage history. No records of performance survive, but if this play is indeed the *Lady Jane* of Henslowe's *Diary,* we must assume from the title page that it was performed by the Earl of Worcester's Men at the Rose Theatre in 1602–3. Certainly, such a play would have been highly topical then, coming just one year after the abortive rebellion of the Earl of Essex against Queen Elizabeth. Since Shakespeare's *Richard II* was perceived as having actionable political significance on that occasion, the 1553 attempt of Sir Thomas Wyatt to place a Protestant successor on the throne of England would also have been titillatingly reminiscent of the events of 1601.[4] In this new play, the refusal of the people of London to support the Earl of Essex is echoed in their spurning of the cause of Sir Thomas Wyatt, albeit that his candidate was a Protestant lady opposing a Catholic queen who wished to make a Spanish marriage. The important thing is that each play indicates the loyalty of Londoners to the Tudors.

Synopsis. As the young King Edward VI lies dying, the Dukes of Suffolk and Northumberland scheme to place their own children on the throne, bypassing the Tudor princesses Mary and Elizabeth in favor of the Protestant Lady Jane Grey, the daughter of Suffolk and wife of Lord Guilford Dudley, son to Northumberland. Sir Thomas Wyatt refuses to approve the so-called will of King Edward favoring this succession (1.1.37) but after Edward's death the dukes proclaim Jane as queen. Jane and her husband, however, do not share their fathers' ambition, Jane in particular preferring a humble life in the company of her spouse to any worldly glory. She fears for their future as they are led for safekeeping to the Tower of London.

Mary is then revealed, dressed in nun-like garb, reading a Roman Catholic prayer book and claiming that the riches within it are more valuable to her than the rule of England. But when Wyatt comes to inform her that Jane has been proclaimed queen she agrees to press her own legitimate claim to the throne. In the meantime, members of the Privy Council attempt to gain unanimous support for Queen Jane, but Wyatt's eloquence in Mary's cause evokes a change of heart in Arundel. He decides to overlook Mary's religious "errors," resolving to support her and to seek the aid of the citizens.

In act 2 Mary is tumultuously proclaimed in the marketplace of Cambridge after two unsuccessful attempts to proclaim Queen Jane. Almost instantly Northumberland is arrested by Arundel and led to the Tower, where he accepts his own fate and hopes for mercy for Jane and his son. Suffolk is betrayed by a servant who, Judas-like, commits suicide. Then, in an ironic Websterian scene, the servant is given a comic obituary by a clown who digs up the blood money and departs to misuse it.

In act 3 Queen Mary, secure in her inheritance, wishes immediate re-establishment of Catholicism in England, declaring herself no longer bound by her earlier oath promising religious freedom (3.1.26–27). Mary adamantly vows to submit Queen Jane and her noble supporters to the full rigors of the law. Wyatt is angered by this vengefulness and infuriated when the Spanish ambassador arrives to arrange for Mary's betrothal to his master, King Philip. Despite Wyatt's objections, Mary announces her determination for the match. This act propels him into rebellion. In the Tower, while Jane and Guilford lament their imprisonment, they hear news of Northumberland's execution and meet Suffolk on his way to the block.

Act 4 is devoted to Wyatt's attempt to block the Spanish marriage. Even in rebellion, Wyatt proves himself to be a noble, chivalrous Protestant warrior, scrupulously observant of the rules of war. At first he garners some support from the populace and even attracts some nobles. However, when London remains loyal to Queen Mary, his followers *"all steale away from* Wyat *and leaue him alone."* He resolves to fight gallantly to the death but the act ends with his wounding and capture.

In act 5 Jane and Guilford are tried for high treason. With touching affection each tries to save the other, and Guilford eloquently disclaims any wish for power. Despite their pleas, each is sentenced, Jane to burning and Guilford to the contumely of hanging, drawing, and quartering. A "merciful" Queen Mary commutes the sentences to beheading. Wyatt is now taken to be executed, noting that "Had *London* kept his word, *Wyat* had stood, / But now King *Phillip* enters through my blood" (5.2.36–37). Jane and Guilford bid each other farewell. In an ironic contrast with the entrance of Queen Mary (1.3), Jane is depicted with her Protestant prayer book, willingly stripping off "this [*sic*] worldly ornaments" (5.2.130) in preparation for death. Even at the last these two innocent souls are unselfish as each wishes to precede the other to the block. But rank has privilege; Jane goes first, and in a macabre touch her head is brought before Guilford as he goes to his own execution, reminding the assembled lords of their innocence: "The Fathers pride has causde the Childrens fall" (5.2.181). The play concludes with the Duke of Norfolk saying that they shall be buried in one grave "as fits their loues."

Critical comments.   Exactly how much the printed version omits of the performance text is perhaps indicated by the title page, for *"the Coronation of Queen Mary,* and the coming in of King Philip" are conspicuously absent. In terms of what may be Webster's contribution, the first and last two scenes of the play seem, on a subjective level, to sound like him, particularly Lady Jane's animadversions on death after the death of King Edward, although one must be wary of allowing Webster a special privilege on that topic. "Alasse, how small an Vrne contains a King " (1.2.2), she says, eloquently perceiving the ironic juxtaposition of Edward's dead march and the procession that leads both her and Dudley to the Tower:

> We are led with pompe to prison.
> O propheticke soule,
> Lo we ascend into our chaires of State,
> Like funerall Coffins, in some funerall pompe
> Descending to their graues . . .
>   (1.2.62–66)

Likewise, her disavowal of majesty, "Who would wear fetters though they were all of golde? " (1.1.25), has something of a Websterian ring.

What looks like evidence of Webster's imitative, "magpie method of composition"[5] also appears very early in the play when Jane's imagery on the death of Edward VI, "quicke lightning, which is no sooner seene, / But is extinct" (1.1.3–4), immediately suggests the balcony scene of *Romeo and Juliet* (2.2.119–20); like them, Jane and Dudley can be united only in the tomb. Similarly there are echoes of Shakespeare's early history plays, which also treat the folly of trusting in humankind and following ambition rather than putting faith in the Almighty. And, following the same pattern, those who choose ill, whether for honest reasons like Wyatt or for ambition like Suffolk and Northumberland, die well after seeing the error of their ways or, in Wyatt's case, professing devotion to the Established Church, as his final words to the Catholic Bishop of Winchester illustrate: "When that houre comes, wherein my blood is split, / My crosse will looke as bright as yours twice guilt" (5.2.23–24).

Even more noteworthy is the treatment of the two reluctant young victims of their fathers' masculine drive to power. With the primary emphasis on Jane, she becomes an echo of her feminine counterparts in Shakespeare's histories who are almost invariably sacrificed to the political machinations of exploitive men. Yet at the same time her character also foreshadows those later tragic Webster heroines, Vittoria and the Duchess of Malfi, used by their relatives for their own ends. Guilford is eloquent in his plea before the Council: "We sought no Kingdome, we desired no Crowne, / It was imposde vpon vs by constraint, / Like goulden fruit hung on a barren Tree" (5.1.69–71). Then, in expressing resignation in the next scene, he delivers a Websterian-sounding sententia: "The world like to a sickell, bends it selfe, / Men runne their course of liues as in a maze, / Our office is to die, yours but to gaze" (5.2.63–65). Jane is the stronger character, an ideal young woman and Protestant foil to the frustrated Roman Catholic Queen Mary, with her desire for both a masterful husband and the Old Faith. Yet both queens are treated with such objectivity that the twin themes of monarchy and legitimacy of religion are juxtaposed, but not judged.

The surviving text offers tantalizing hints of what the original might have been. Certainly some of the vigorous scenes with Captain Brett and his Londoners (probably written by Dekker), indicate that a large procession might have been included. But all this can be no more than speculation. The first two scenes and the two concluding ones, with their macabre touches, hint at Webster's authorship, but we cannot be certain.

Further Works of 1602–3

Henslowe's *Diary* records a payment on 2 November 1602 as an advance to Henry Chettle, Thomas Middleton, and John Webster for a new play entitled *Christmas Comes but Once a Year*. Now lost, nothing of it is known except that it must have been designed for the seasonal theatrical trade. It was apparently performed by the Earl of Worcester's Men at the Rose during Christmas 1602–3, since Henslowe notes payments for costumes on 23 and 26 November 1602. In the same year Webster wrote prefatory verses to Anthony Munday's *The Palmerin of England*.

Collaboration with John Marston: *The Malcontent*

Date, text, and authorship. John Webster surfaces again in 1604 on the title page of the third quarto edition of *The Malcontent* by John Marston (written 1602–4), which reads:

THE / MALCONTENT. / *Augmented by Marston.* / With the Additions played by the Kinges / Maiesties servants. / Written by Ihon Webster. / [Ornament] / 1604. / at London / Printed by V[alentine]. S[ims]. for William Aspley, and / are to be sold at his shop in Paules / Church-yard.

However, the heading of the *Induction* indicates an apparent contradiction: "THE INDVCTION TO / THE MALECONTENT, AND / the additions acted by the Kings Ma- / iesties servants. / Written by *John Webster*." This questions what share Webster had in the addition of some six hundred lines to the Blackfriars Theatre text to increase the length to that customary in a public theatre. Webster almost certainly wrote the *Induction,* but there is some speculation about his other possible contributions to the augmentation of the play.[6] Recent work by both G. K. Hunter and D. J. Lake indicates that the new role of the clown Passarello is by Webster, who apparently took his material from current jestbooks, while the railing character of Bilioso and sundry minor additions are by Marston.[7]

Stage history. The *Induction* is designed to introduce *The Malcontent* as a new kind of play and to justify its performance by the adult company of the Globe rather than by the children's troupe at Blackfriars for which it was originally designed. The colloquy between Sly and Condell exploits this fact by offering a suggestion of illegality, claiming that the text was pirated from Blackfriars as vengeance for the boy players' appropriation of Thomas Kyd's *The Spanish Tragedy*. This, of course, is really nothing more than advertising publicity, since both texts were already in print and therefore available for performance by any company.

Considerable changes were necessary to adapt the play to Globe specifications [the play was *both* cut & expanded] where songs, musical introductions, and entr'actes were not customary. Consequently, the original play was now too short by the length of the *Induction* and the additions that Marston and Webster supplied. Further, the audience at the public theater was less sophisticated than that at the private playhouse, and the new satiric style of the play was an unusual venture for this adult company, while the bitter, astringent quality of the central character, Duke Altofronto, disguised as the malcontent Malevole, was absolutely new. Therefore the *Induction* was carefully composed to prepare the public audience, to lead it into this new world of moral tragicomedy.

One may legitimately wonder why the King's Men decided on such an innovation. But this was an opportune moment, for the company was just reopening for business after a plague year, and its audience, after a theatrical drought, might well have been ready for a new dramatic experience. In addition, success in this mode would then contribute to an increased repertory by facilitating transference of similar plays from the coterie theaters to the public theaters.

Synopsis. The *Induction* by John Webster includes actors of the King's Men appearing in their own persons, among them three who later created roles in *The Duchess of Malfi*. The most famous of these is Richard Burbage, notable for his Shakespearean roles of Richard III, Hamlet, Othello, and King Lear, as well as Webster's Ferdinand. Also appearing is Henry Condell, who originated the role of the Cardinal, but is better remembered for his collaboration with John Heminges in editing Shakespeare's First Folio (1623). Third is John Lowin, the original Bosola. William Sly, John Sincklo, and an unidentified "Tyreman" round out the cast.

In this highly sophisticated *Induction,* Webster uses Sly as a stalking horse. He is the expert witness, already familiar with the original performance, who raises a variety of objections to the presentation of a coterie theater play before a public audience so that Webster can refute them. Sly discusses the nature of the drama with Condell, who insists that it is not bitter, "neither satire nor moral, but the mean passage of a history" (ll.51–52), an entertainment—in other words, a tragicomedy. Sly complains about being refused a seat on the stage (a practice allowed in private theaters) and insists that Richard Burbage cannot play the main character as efficiently as the boy player he has already seen. At this, Lowin leads him and Sincklo to a "private room" from which they may view the play. But in fact the actors go to costume themselves for their assigned roles in the performance.

The play itself concerns the ultimately successful attempt of Altofronto, the virtuous deposed Duke of Genoa, to regain his throne and wife, as well as to restore order to his state. In order to attain these ends he infiltrates the decadent court of the usurper Duke Pietro Jacomo and his wife, the lustful Aurelia, disguised as Malevole, a bitter-tongued railer. His anger is so general that he is not taken seriously when he continually denounces flattery, lechery, infidelity, adultery, and "distemperance," vices that are personified by individual members of the court. He appears willing to perform any service for Duke Pietro Jacomo but, in fact, works against his supplanter with slow but steady patience.

The court is indeed totally corrupt: both the usurper Duke and his wife, Aurelia, have minions, and Maquerelle, an old panderess, arranges sexual assignations. Two other characters are added to the original play: Bilioso, a stupid marshal whose name speaks for itself, and his fool, Passarello. The first continually rails while the second (probably invented by Webster) engages in moral comment masked by jests and witticisms. They echo the relentlessly hostile denunciations of Altofronto on a more obvious, comic level. The one wholly virtuous character of the play is Maria, the imprisoned wife of Altofronto, whose honor remains proof against all assaults.

Discovering Aurelia and Ferneze, her minion, in bed, Pietro seeks vengeance, not knowing that his duchess is already plotting against his own life, partly to preserve her reputation but also so that she and Mendoza, a courtier who has wounded Ferneze, can marry and supplant him. But Mendoza's secret plan is to marry Maria, the imprisoned wife of Altofronto / Malevole. Working as a double agent, Malevole informs Pietro of the plot against him and suggests that he hide out as a hermit. Pietro as hermit returns and interrupts an evening of court merrymaking to announce his own "suicide" because of his sorrow at Aurelia's misconduct.

Mendoza, in accordance with Pietro's expressed wish, is named Duke of Genoa, while all await word from the Duke of Florence. Bilioso bears Florence's decision that his daughter Aurelia must die, Pietro must be banished for his part in the plot against Altofronto, and the deposed duke restored. This sentence leads Pietro / Hermit to repent and promise to live a solitary and penitent life. At this Malevole reveals his true identity to Pietro, Celso, a faithful friend, and Ferneze (who was believed to have died). They all unite to plot the downfall of Mendoza.

Aurelia is deservedly banished, but misfortune brings her to confess her repentance to her disguised husband, the hermit. In act 5 Malevole / Altofronto, apparently obeying the orders of Mendoza, arranges to bring Maria to the usurper while she prays for the strength to remain faithful to her beloved Altofronto. There are no limits to Mendoza's wickedness, and when Malevole announces (falsely) that he has killed the "Hermit," Mendoza forces him to inhale the "poison" he has had Malevole supply. Malevole appears to fall dead and Celso is ordered to bury him.

That evening Mendoza holds a masque, and in the course of the entertainment the disguised Altofronto/Malevole and Pietro both dance with their respective wives, Maria and Aurelia, where they hear expressions of love for themselves, and, repentance in the case of Aurelia. With everyone off guard, Altofronto and Pietro privately reveal themselves to their ladies and after another dancing measure, they and their assistants publicly unmask, surround Mendoza with drawn pistols, and seize him. The plotter begs cravenly for his life, which the restored Duke Altofronto contemptuously grants.

Critical comments. Although John Webster had a relatively small part in the writing and revision of *The Malcontent,* his work with John Marston was to prove an important dramaturgical influence. To begin with, the scene is laid in Italy, that country stereotyped by English Renaissance playwrights as a sink of iniquity, the epitome of depravity, the home of murder, rape, and corruption both religious and sexual. The play also demonstrates the same kind of intrigue, sudden shifts of mood, reversals of situation, effective juxtaposition, and amorality, here used for moral ends, that Webster was later to use. In some ways also the emphasis on dramatic unreality with a tragicomic ending leads one irresistibly toward *The Devil's Law-Case,* while the masquelike conclusion foreshadows "the Masque of Madmen" in *The Duchess of Malfi.*

The deliberate artificiality of this play would have been more suited to the private theater than the public playhouse, because the use of adolescent male actors would automatically cause intellectual detachment. The audience would thus be forced to deal with the matter and form of the play rather than the quasirealistic impersonation of characters by adult actors. This alteration of perception arises most particularly with the role of Altofronto: in a children's company the intellectual and moral content of his railing would be more important than the actor's physical embodiment of the role. In addition, the structure of the play with its emphasis on spiritual as well as physical masking, and the masquelike conclusion of the action through dance, would have been more palatable to a sophisticated, intellectual audience accustomed to word games and sudden shifts, than to the popular, literal-minded clientele.[8]

Thus the *Induction* serves the important purpose of preparing the "audience psychologically, aesthetically, and intellectually for the new kind of dramatic experience" they are about to undergo, while giving them an additional perspective on the events of the play.[9] Simultaneously, it contributes to the circular structure to the play by reversing the masquelike conclusion of the action that is an important bridge from the fictional to the quotidian world. As the *Induction* prepares the audience for artificiality, underscored by discordant music to emphasize the amorality of the Genoese court, so the return to moral order is accompanied by melodious music and the contrivance of a revelatory masque that reflects the entire play as satiric entertainment. With the epilogue, the characters of the play resume their original personae. Like Shakespeare's Duke of Vienna in *Measure for Measure,* Altofronto has brought the characters of the play to moral reawakening. Virtue triumphs, evil sees its true nature and repents, and despite near tragedy, the play ends with a restoration of order.[10]

Observed in this manner the *Induction* adds an additional perspective to a play that becomes "an intricate metaphor for the actual world,"[11] but with a more optimistic attitude than Webster was himself to show in his own later, independent plays. Doubtless Marston's own emerging religious convictions led him to conclude a beneficent force in the universe, a constant moral center, something that Webster finds darkly doubtful in *The White Devil, The Duchess of Malfi,* and even *The Devil's Law-Case.* Certainly Webster learned much from Marston in terms of dramatic structure, but in his poetic talent, sympathy, and vision of both the inherent tragedy and despairing dignity of human existence, he transcended his mentor.

Collaborations with Thomas Dekker in 1604–5: *Westward Ho!* and *Northward Ho!*

Date, text, and authorship. During 1604–5 John Webster worked with Thomas Dekker on two citizen comedies written for the Children of Paul's. These plays are frequently slighted in histories of

English drama and discussions of citizen comedy because of the merry theatrical war precipitated by *Westward Ho!*. Almost immediately, the consortium of George Chapman, Ben Jonson, and John Marston replied with *Eastward Ho!*, a play on the prodigal son motif that includes satire on King James and his Scottish subjects, which promptly landed the authors in prison. This play was written for the rival children's company, the Children of the Queen's Revels, playing at the Blackfriars Theatre, the same company that had introduced *The Malcontent*.

With equal speed, Dekker and Webster replied with *Northward Ho!*, which also makes some use of the prodigal son theme and gently satirizes Chapman. Quite clearly this was a merry altercation rather than a repetition of the so-called War of the Theatres (1600–1601), also between the two rival children's companies, in which Marston threatened violence on Ben Jonson. Unfortunately for Dekker and Webster (who was writing for a boy company for the first time), the reply from their rivals was so manifestly superior to either of their own efforts that only *Eastward Ho!* has achieved canonical status, leaving Dekker's and Webster's plays almost totally forgotten.[12]

Both these plays were published by different printers in the same year, 1607, after the dissolution of the Children of Paul's as an acting company; following critical custom, they will be treated together.

The title page of *Westward Ho!* reads as follows:

VVEST-VVARD / HOE. / *As it hath beene diuers times Acted / by the Children of Paules.* Written by Tho: Decker and / Iohn Webster. / [Ornament of William Jaggard] / Printed at London, and to be sold by Iohn Hodgets / dwelling in Paules Churchyard / 1607 / [.]

This play was originally entered in the *Stationers' Register* on 2 March 1605, with the notation that the printer, Henry Rockett, needed sufficient authority to publish it. The entry is later crossed out, presumably because the Children of Paul's did not wish to release the copy. The text as finally printed appears to come from the original manuscript, the "foul papers," of the authors, but apart from some careless typesetting, it is a good one.[13]

The title page of *Northward Ho!* reads as follows:

NORTH-VVARD / HOE. *Sundry times Acted by the Children / of Paules.* By Thomas Decker, and / Iohn VVebster. [Ornament] Imprinted at London by G. Eld. / 1607.

This play was entered in the *Stationers' Register* for printing by George Eld on 6 August 1607, and publication ensued almost immediately. As with its companion piece, the text appears to have been released for printing as a result of the dissolution of the Children of Paul's, but the nature of that text, whether foul papers or fair copy, is not clear. The published text appears to be a good one, with any difficulties arising from the nature of the manuscript.[14]

There are no sources for either play as a whole, although some situations in *Westward Ho!* recall the *Satiromastix* of Dekker, and the tale of the lost ring in *Northward Ho!* may come from the sixty-second story in La Sale's *Cent Nouvelles Nouvelles.*[15]

Synopses. In *Westward Ho!* the scene is London, where Mistress Justiniano, believing herself abandoned by her bankrupt Italian husband, follows the advice of Mistress Birdlime, a bawd, and agrees to become the mistress of an unnamed earl. This decision is not easy for the lady, but she believes it to be her only alternative. The implied social comment is obvious: what else can a penniless woman do to save herself from starvation? However, when she meets the Earl in act 2 he is so old and unappetizing that she cannot go through with the proposition, although she does beg money from him to pay Justiniano's debts.

The other plot of the play concerns Master Justiniano, the lady's husband. He is the stereotypical jealous Italian, so certain that his wife has cuckolded him that he says he will leave England. But first, he cynically wishes to test the chastity of other city wives, and disguises himself as Master Parenthesis, a writing teacher, hiring himself out to teach Mistress Honeysuckle and, later, Mistresses Wafer and Tenterhook. Their aim is to write to the gallants who are importuning them, and Justiniano expects them to be unfaithful to their husbands. Another social comment is implied here, since the wives have never been taught how to write.

The gallants, Sir Gosling Glowworm (a drunkard, as his name implies), Linstock, and Whirlpool, accompanied by Sergeant Ambush, all decide to go to Brainford to meet the ladies in an assignation. But Justiniano has not yet finished with the Earl. The Italian appears disguised in his wife's clothes, and brings the nobleman to repent for his lustful desires by showing him the ugly face of this "woman" he has tried to seduce. Then Justiniano reveals himself, claiming he has poisoned his wife to save her honor. He draws a curtain and shows her apparently dead. The Earl is appalled and repents his sensuality and his part in her death, as the three London husbands, Tenterhook,

Honeysuckle, and Wafer, look on. Suddenly, to general rejoicing, she is revealed as living. At this moment, Justiniano praises her virtue and tells the husbands that their wives are currently cuckolding them in Brainford. Immediately, the three men set out for the town, ready to catch them in their deceit.

The final act of the play shows the three women in Brainford where, since flirtation is their only aim, they avoid going to bed with their importunate gallants by inventing a series of ruses to keep the men at bay. The case of Monopoly, who is refused because he smells of tobacco and is forced to smoke two rooms away from the sensitive ladies, has a surprising modernity. The husbands then arrive and discover their old friend, the bawd Birdlime, and her assistant, Luce. Eventually the wives are proved chaste, and the gallants are discomfited, while the husbands are chagrined at being unmasked as regular visitors to Mistress Birdlime's establishment. Both wives and husbands now turn on Birdlime, who promptly takes oars for London. Justiniano delivers a moralistic speech summing up the action, saying that it has all been a merriment and starts the movement toward general reconciliation and forgiveness by kissing his own wife. News comes that the foolish guzzler, Sir Gosling Glowworm, has had his head broken, and with laughter and general forgiveness the couples embark for London as the play ends with a waterman's song.

Northward Ho! is in tune with its predecessor, but at the same time it reacts against *Eastward Ho!*, the play written in reply for the Children of the Queen's Revels. This time the young gallant, Luke Greenshield, attempts to seduce Mistress Mayberry, but is refused by the chaste lady. Angered by this, he tells her husband and the poet Bellamont that he and Master Fetherstone have both lain with her. Greenshield presents a ring as proof and also lets fall the name of the lady, pretending that he and Fetherstone are not aware of Mayberry's identity. Masking his anger, Mayberry asks for the ring (which had been his gift to his wife) and returns to London to confront her.

Mayberry and Bellamont accuse the wife, who speedily convinces them of her own innocence, with the result that Mayberry forgives her and swears to take bloodless vengeance on Greenshield. Two subplots now surface. In one, the bawd Doll, who has had her brothel broken up by law, decides to put herself under the protection of one Hornet and open an establishment in a fashionable section of London. She spends the remainder of the play trying to finance her enterprise. In the second subplot, Philip, the prodigal son of Bellamont, the poet, is arrested for debt, and his father decides to bail him out for £80, swearing that this will be the last time. In a further complication, Luke Greenshield is revealed as already married to Kate, whom he has neglected. At one point he shamelessly brings her to reside in the Mayberry household, introducing her as his sister. Quite naturally, she wishes to repay him in kind by pretending to have an affair with Fetherstone.

During these developments there are scenes in Dutch- and Welsh-fractured English, and, in addition, satire at the expense of Bellamont. This character is really a parodic portrait of George Chapman, one of the authors of *Eastward Ho!*. He is shown as a serious poet trying to write a classical tragedy, and also being importuned by the Welsh Captain Jenkins to write a love song to Doll. When Doll comes to him, Bellamont tries to seduce her, despite her reluctance because of his age. Then, after the Welsh captain reveals himself, Bellamont throws Doll out, ignoring her protestations of repentance. This contretemps does not prevent the shrewd businesswoman from continuing her attempts to raise money for her new venture.

Mayberry invites Bellamont to come with him to Ware, claiming that he has a comedy for the poet to write and the plot lies there. Fetherstone and Kate are already on their way, and Mayberry sends his wife on ahead, certain that Greenshield will follow and find himself a cuckold. The entire group of male travelers eventually gathers, and on the way they decide, in a parody of *The Canterbury Tales,* to play jokes on each other. The victim of the best joke will pay the expenses of the final dinner. This gives Greenshield a chance to simulate Bellamont's commitment to Bedlam, with an ensuing mad scene.

On arrival at Ware, Bellamont deliberately brings Mayberry to the wrong inn. He also promises to get Mayberry a lady to comfort him, sending Greenshield to collect the "Yorkshire lady" from next door. She is Kate Greenshield disguised. At first her husband does not recognize her as he warmly solicits her for Mayberry. When he discovers her identity he is mightily chagrined and Bellamont taunts him with the humiliations he had planned for Mayberry. Husbands and wives are reconciled and the final jest is to trick Fetherstone into marrying Doll, a fate the empty-headed young man accepts with resignation.

Critical comments.   *Westward Ho!* takes its title from the Thames watermen's cry indicating passage from the London side to the west bank; it also possessed the proverbial meaning of crossing the river to such towns at Brainford (modern Brentford) for sexual assignations.[16]

The title of the play thus clearly telegraphs its content to the audience—
a London-based comedy full of sexual intrigue and attempted seduction
with a basically moral outcome. In a similar manner the geographical
titles of the other *Ho!* plays indicate to some extent their themes.
Eastward Ho! suggests the City itself and the Court in particular, a
dangerous satiric topic, as its authors discovered. *Northward Ho!,* on
the other hand, indicates a journey to the town of Ware, the home of
the famous Great Bed, allegedly large enough to hold four couples.[17]

Northward Ho! follows much the same pattern as its predecessor,
building through a series of complications and quasivaudeville turns to
a grand confrontation in which everything is sorted out. As before, it
is an automatic response in both plays for husbands to believe immediately in the dishonesty of their wives. The play does, however,
differ from *Westward Ho!* in its looser plotting since it lacks a controlling
character like Justiniano. Instead it reacts to *Eastward Ho!,* the play
of its rival company, in using the same prodigal son theme, and also
in the genial satire of Chapman as Bellamont.[18] This undoubtedly
dramatizes Chapman's known desire to be poet laureate, a post in
which skill in the writing of "occasional" poems is essential. A further
reaction to *Eastward Ho!* may also be perceived in the use of dialect.
Where the rival play made fun of "carpet knights" and Scottish nobles,
Dekker and Webster exploit the linguistic problems of the Dutch and
Welsh for the purposes of bawdy mispronunciation and misinterpretation.
Since Dekker was apparently of Dutch extraction, such carefully developed interpolations are frequent in his plays, but here the authors
seem to exploit the facility of the Children of Paul's in a series of
bravura pieces that are funny in themselves but do not advance the
plot. Throughout each play changes are rung on suggestive double
meanings, and *Westward Ho!* has a virtuoso interlude when Parenthesis (the disguised Justiniano) delivers an alphabet of bawdry from
A to V.

Justiniano gives unity to his play and he repeatedly recalls the
manipulative Vice of medieval drama. He is both the stereotypical
jealous Italian and the moral arbiter of the play, despite his cynicism
about the virtue of English women. But what is most remarkable in
these two plays is the tone of cool, nonjudgmental detachment and
artificiality that pervades them. Situations are obviously contrived, and
coincidences occur without any evident concern for motivation or character
development.

Sex forms the basis of the action, but there is a curious attitude toward morality. The women are flirtatious but invariably honest, while the double standard is tacitly approved. When in *Westward Ho!* the women discover that their husbands have been Birdlime's customers, for instance, they accept the situation with astonishing equanamity: "Haue we smelt you out foxes" (5.4.236). The nearest thing to rebuke comes from Mistress Tenterhook: "Doe you come after vs with hue and cry when you are the theeues your Selues?" (5.4.237–38). The men, however, are less tolerant and more suspicious. *Northward Ho!*, however, does have a slight differentiation in that Luke Greenshield treats his wife abominably and is tricked quite skillfully as a punishment. Adultery is depicted as the proper comic fate for a bad husband, and no one feels sorry for this reprehensible young man.[19] Similarly, the rake Fetherstone accepts his marriage to the bawd, Doll, as inevitable, and he seems quite prepared to make some capital out of her entrepreneurial skills.

Both these plays also exploit the economic basis of citizen comedy. They portray acquisitiveness and expenditure as dominant preoccupations of such folk as apprentices, shopkeepers, craftsmen, and small businessmen in homes, inns, shops, and brothels. The plays are also replete with implied social commentary and re-create the life of everyday London. Women chafe at their inferior status, resenting the authority of their husbands. And one must not forget that a married woman was a *femme couverte,* one whose legal personality was subsumed by that of her husband, who controlled her property and even her life. It was still legally permissible for him to beat her (using a rod no thicker than a thumb—hence the term "rule of thumb"), although this practice was discouraged since it was likely to destroy friendship between husband and wife.

Yet feminine independence was asserted by women of the upper and citizen classes in habitually refusing to nurse their children themselves, sending them instead to lower-class wet nurses. In *Westward Ho!* Mistress Honeysuckle (an apt name) complains that a husband's wish for his wife to undertake this maternal duty is "the policy of husbands to keepe their Wiues in" (1.2.116–17). Overall, the women of citizen comedy offer a fine contribution to English Renaissance feminism. They are a singularly resourceful crew of skillful plotters, jealous of their honor, and capable of outwitting their sometimes foolish husbands. The general premise is that intelligent women will always be able to finesse the sexual advances of randy young gallants; similarly, suspicious husbands will get their comeuppance and be ridiculed for their folly. Their motto would indeed seem to be: "O the wit of a woman when she is put to the pinch" (*WH*, 3.1.44–45). Curiously, young lovers appear infrequently; in general the characters of these plays are those whose marriage is past its early years. Long habit may have given rise to ennui and suspicion of sexual experimentation on the part of both wives and husbands.

Exactly how much Webster contributed to both these plays is open to question, and some earlier critics have dismissed his share as minimal. Lucas, in fact, omitted both these plays as well as *Sir Thomas Wyatt* from his edition, relegating discussion of the Dekker collaborations to an appendix.[20] More recently, Peter B. Murray gives about forty percent of each play to Webster, "the first and third of a total of four parts of *Westward Ho* [*sic*] and the first, third, and fifth parts of a total of six for *Northward Ho* [*sic*]."[21] As he notes, this apportionment jibes well with what is known of Webster's notoriously slow composition, so that Dekker was left free to gallop ahead while his collaborator brought up the rear, plodding along at his own pace, and the two joined forces for the conclusion. General agreement among textual critics suggests Dekker as the guiding spirit of both plays, and assigns to him the overall plotting.

Webster learned a great deal from these experiments in citizen comedy, particularly in his depiction of intelligent and resourceful women, both mature and married, something that distinguishes all his independent plays. From the discrete approach of *Northward Ho!* he may also have come to a further understanding of the importance of contrasting scenes, the turning aside from the main plot for independent exploitation of a situation. In addition, the resurrection of Flamineo in *The White Devil* may owe something to *Westward Ho!* and its revivification of Mistress Justiniano. The display of the wax figure of Antonio in *The Duchess of Malfi* may also have its genesis in the same scene, while the Bedlam scene in *Northward Ho!* with its jest against Bellamont foreshadows "the Masque of Madmen" brought by Bosola to torture the Duchess.[22] The use of word play is something else he continued throughout his career, and the coolly amoral tone of *The Devil's Law-Case* has a great deal in common with the two *Ho!* plays. As usual, one may say that no experience was lost on John Webster, and that he proceeded to transmute it into something different and distinctive, yet reminiscent of its origin.

With an introductory poem to *Arches of Triumph* (1604), a volume published to memorialize the entry of James I into London, the apprentice period of Webster's poetic and dramatic career comes to an end. Throughout this period of his career Webster had written little identifiable work, although the *Induction* to *The Malcontent* demonstrates a mature and thoughtful analysis of the nature of dramatic illusion and the craft of the actor, together with the importance of audience acceptance, a constant concern of this thoroughly professional playwright.

Chapter Three
The White Devil

The White Devil is Webster's first independently written play and one of the two tragedies on which his reputation as a major dramatist rests. From his experience as collaborator and writer of dedications and tributes, he suddenly emerges as a mature playwright with a unique sense of structure and a highly personal vision of the universe. He makes use of his legal training in his depiction of the arraignment of his heroine, Vittoria Corombona, and breaks new ground in making such a resourceful woman the center of the tragic action, a practice he was to repeat in his greatest play, *The Duchess of Malfi*. Webster's apprenticeship was now over, and the product of his self-criticized slowness of composition was brought to light. Although he lamented the theatrical failure of *The White Devil*, he looked also to the appreciation of his readers, believing that he had written for posterity, not merely for the passing moment of performance.[1] And he was right.

Text

The title page of the First Quarto (1612) reads as follows:

THE WHITE DIVEL, / OR, / The Tragedy of *Paulo Giordano / Ursini*, Duke of *Brachiano*, / With / The Life and Death of Vittoria / Corombona the famous / Venetian Curtizan. / *Acted by the Queenes Maiesties Servants.* / Written by Iohn Webster. / *Non inferiora secutus.* / LONDON, / Printed by N[icholas]. O[kes]. for *Thomas Archer*, and are to be sold / at his Shop in Popes head Pallace, neere the / Royall Exchange. 1612.

The text of this play is free from major errors. It lacks act and scene divisions. Bibliographic scholars conclude that the manuscript supplied to the printer, close to the original draft, was revised by Webster for publication.[2] It was not one that had been used by the players, for it does not have detailed stage directions, and some it does have are incorrect, as if the author had worked without the theater text in front of him. Corrections were made in press; some indicating that they come either from another manuscript or from the author. In view of recent discoveries concerning Webster and his residence in London this possibility seems nearly certain, since Nicholas Okes, the printer of Webster's three independent works, was a Smithfield neighbor. Other quarto editions followed in 1631, 1665, and 1672.

Date

The publication date is 1612, but the address to the reader indicates that *The White Devil* had already been unsuccessfully performed. Some parameters can be ascertained from the internal evidence of borrowings from Robert Tofte's *Honour's Academy* (1610) and a reference by Thomas Dekker (in the dedication to his own play, *If It Be Not Good, the Devil Is in It,* printed 1612) to a forthcoming play by a "worthy friend" (presumably his former collaborator, Webster). Considering Webster's slow and careful habit of composition, scholars conclude that the play was mostly written over a period of some two years, 1608–10.[3]

Stage History

The White Devil was first performed by the Queen's Men at the Red Bull Theatre probably in January or February of 1612.[4] According to Webster's own introduction to the published text of the play, it was a failure, due to the inclemency of the weather, the darkness of the theater, and—probably most of all—an unappreciative, uncomprehending audience. The players, however, were not to blame; at the end of the Second Quarto of 1631 Webster recalls with praise the "well approved industry of my friend Master [Richard] Perkins [as Flamineo], and confess [that] the worth of his action did crown both the beginning and the end." This same edition indicates the play had been "diuers times Acted, by the Queenes Maiesties Seruants at the Phoenix, in Drury Lane"; this theater, originally known as the Cockpit, had been redesigned by Inigo Jones and then renamed in hopes of attracting an upper-class clientele. The Queen's Men had moved into these new premises in 1617, abandoning the Red Bull, with its more heterogeneous and unsophisticated audience.

By the time of the Third Quarto, in 1665, it was noted as being acted at the Theatre-Royal, and in 1672 it was still being performed there by the King's Men. Samuel Pepys, the diarist, disliked both his seat and the play in 1661, and a second visit did not change his opinion. However, Gerard Langbaine, in his *Account of the English Dramatic Poets* (1691), found Webster's *The White Devil, The Duchess of Malfi,* and *Appius and Virginia* successful "even in our age," while John Downes, in his *Roscius Anglicanus* (1708), noted that the play had been well received in its own day.

The eighteenth and nineteenth centuries are barren of performances, but in 1707, Nahum Tate, the redoubtable adapter of Elizabethan and Jacobean plays, printed his unstaged version of *The White Devil* under the title *Injur'd Love: Or, The Cruel Husband.* The emphasis is on the lust of Duke Paolo, while Vittoria, though listed in the dramatic personae as "The Court-Mistress," is now pure and loyal to Camillo as she attempts to dissuade Brachiano from marrying her. The attempt to moralize the play and gain pathos by stressing the young son of Isabella, together with a strengthened renunciation scene between Brachiano and his wife, splinters the focus of the action. Cornelia's superb burial poem is omitted, as is the parody of extreme unction. Even Vittoria loses her distinctive strength and forthrightness in the pedestrian verse, while the kindest thing one can say about the epilogue is that it is simplistic, with references to "Our wanton Wife, and Devil of a Wife" and to a husband "Doom'd by just Fate to die of raving Fits, / To fright ill-natur'd Husbands to their Wits."[5]

The twentieth century has seen numerous performances and a tradition of performing the play in modern dress. Important London productions were those of 1925, by the Renaissance Theatre at the Scala; of 1935, by the Phoenix Society at St. Martin's; and of 1947, at the Duchess Theatre, where it ran for several months. In 1969 the National Theatre, with Frank Dunlop as producer, mounted the play at the Old Vic, where it ran for nearly a year. Both period costuming and sets were universally praised. It was again revived, to lukewarm reviews, by the National Theatre in 1976 in modern dress, with Glenda Jackson as Vittoria and Jack Shepherd as Flamineo.

The first recorded professional twentieth-century production in the United States was a showcase performance by the Equity Library Theatre, New York, during the 1946–47 season. The next two New York performances came in 1955 in modern dress and without scenery as Monday night "Side-Shows" by the Off-Broadway Phoenix Theatre, directed by Jack Landau, where the melodramatic aspects were stressed. Landau repeated this production in 1965 at the Circle in the Square, where it ran for 152 performances. At the Tyrone Guthrie Theatre, Minneapolis, the play was set in the 1930s gangster era of Chicago.

The modernity of the play was also exploited by Michael Kahn in 1979 when he produced it in "punk rock" style, evoking the late 1960s period of drugs and violence.[6] In general, though there have been numerous regional and nonprofessional productions, *The White Devil* is admired more in the study than on the stage, though portions of it still retain great power over an audience. Webster, in this frequently admired work, has not proved to be good box office, largely because the audience has difficulty with its language, disjunctive scenes, complicated plotting, and constantly shifting perspective. Unfortunately, modern audiences tend to laugh at the astonishing proliferation of deaths rather than perceive the more serious aspects of life that Webster clearly intended to impart on his viewers.

Sources

In *The White Devil* Webster retold an Italian scandal of adultery and murder in high places, involving such well-known Italian noble families as the Medici and the Orsini. The historical Vittoria Accoramboroni was born in Gubbio, Northern Italy, on 15 February 1557, the last of eleven children. She was a young girl of astounding beauty, and therefore her parents took her to Rome to advance her socioeconomic status by making a brilliant marriage. At the age of sixteen she married the young Francesco Peretti, nephew of Cardinal Montalto. The couple went to live in the austere Cardinal's house where Vittoria's extravagance and love of gaiety were unwelcome and her unhappiness increased. Eight years later, on 16 April 1581, Peretti was first shot and then stabbed on a Roman street.

During her marriage, Vittoria had met Paolo Giordano Orsini, Duke of Bracciano. Some twenty years older than her, he had been married since 1558 to Isabella de Medici, sister of the Duke of Florence; the couple had three children.[7] Unlike Webster's character, Isabella had a young lover, Troilo Orsino, from whose company her husband removed her in July 1576. A few weeks later Isabella fell dead while washing her hair (according to the official story). Her lover was shot and killed in Paris the following year. At the time of these events Paolo's confidential chamberlain was Vittoria's brother, Marcello.

In 1581 the widowed Vittoria secretly married Paolo, Duke of Bracciano, *per verba de praesenti,* in words of the present tense. This clandestine union was valid but illegal and required recelebration in a church service to set matters right.[8] Pope Gregory XIII ordered the couple to separate, and then imprisoned Vittoria in the Castel Sant' Angelo (December 1581). In June 1582 Paolo promised he would not see Vittoria again and wrote her a letter of renunciation, on receipt of which she attempted suicide. In November 1582 Vittoria made a similar promise of renunciation and was released.

But the lovers persisted, and on 10 October 1583 they remarried before witnesses in Bracciano. Within a year Paolo developed a malignant leg ulcer that was exacerbated by his pathological corpulence. In December 1584 they returned to Rome, and in February 1585 their marriage in Bracciano was revealed. Again they incurred papal wrath, but Gregory XIII died suddenly just as he was about to order their separation. To prevent the next pope from separating them, the lovers promptly remarried during the Electoral Conclave (April 1585), but within an hour of the ceremony the redoubtable uncle of the murdered Francesco Peretti, Cardinal Montalto, was elected pope, taking the name of Sixtus V.[9] Paolo sought forgiveness of the new pontiff who ordered him to separate from Vittoria.

With this, the couple went north to Venice and thence to Padua, seeking a cure for Paolo's ulcerous leg, but he died, probably of natural causes, at Salò on Lake Garda, 13 November 1585. Vittoria was left a wealthy widow, but she had enemies among the family of Paolo's first wife, Isabella de Medici, who had gained custody of the child Virginio, inheritor of the rest of Paolo's lands and wealth. The Florentine relatives tried to get Vittoria to settle with them, but she retained that large part of her husband's wealth situated in Padua.

The Florentines, however, remained bent on acquisitive vengeance and on the night of 22–23 December 1585, an enemy of Vittoria, Lodovico Orsini, who was also a young relative of Paolo, brought a group of banditti to besiege her house in Padua. Flamineo, her youngest brother, was killed, and Vittoria brutally murdered by Tolomeo Visconti, a hired assassin, who jested as he worked the knife in her bosom asking if he had found her heart. She was praying as she died. Lodovico Orsini, the perpetrator of over forty murders in his thirty-four years, was in turn besieged in his house, and surrendered on Christmas Day. Though technically innocent of the murder of Vittoria, he was imprisoned and strangled two days later. A number of his banditti were also executed. Marcello, the brother of Vittoria, was beheaded by order of Pope Sixtus V in June 1586 for his alleged role in the slaying of the Pope's nephew, Vittoria's first husband.

Webster's available sources for these bloody and violent events have been extensively studied by Gunnar Boklund who, after examining 109 extant manuscripts, eventually limited the possible versions to four.[10] Clearly, Webster used more than one source, but the most probable seems to be an account in one of the newsletters of the Fugger Banking house of Augsburg, for the information of clients and staff in other countries. Boklund makes "a timid plea for the acceptance of MS 8959 (Nationalbibliothek, Vienna),"[11] a version that seems to have been based on a lost Italian source. A second source, particularly for information concerning the papal conclave scenes, was "*A Letter Lately Written from Rome,* by an Italian Gentleman to a Freend of His in Lyons in Fraunce" (1585), a translation by John Florio of a French text by Jérome Bignon. The death scene in which the Duke is taunted by two villains disguised as friars comes from Erasmus's colloquy, "The Funeral" (*Funus,* 1526). In addition, Webster may have had access to other Italian accounts for different aspects of characters and events. In other words the number of putative sources is legion,[12] and the possibility remains that the playwright could even have had some hearsay information, since the events had occurred only twenty-seven years before the play's publication.

Whether John Webster was acquainted with all of these details is not known, but certainly he reinterpreted facts. He does not mention the matrimonial ambition of Tarquinia Accoramboni, Vittoria's mother, as he rewrites her into the moral character of Cornelia, and confuses Marcello, her older brother, with the younger Flamineo who perished with his sister. He also makes both brothers of an age, and invents the fratricide of act 5. Webster probably had no idea of the appearance of Paolo, Duke of Bracciano, and transfers his corpulence to the character of Francisco de Medici, who is largely the playwright's creation. He also makes use of stock figures, particularly the implacable Cardinal Montalto, later Pope, who becomes the typically wicked Italianate churchman. In Zanche, the Moor, he replaces Vittoria's Bolognese maid with the stock figure of the wicked infidel, one who in her blackness serves as a foil for Vittoria, that white devil whose brightness masquerades as virtue.

In his portrait of Vittoria, Webster emphasizes her wickedness, taking up the suggestion in several accounts that she was the instigator of the murders of Francisco Peretti and Isabella de Medici, who is now sanctified into an unselfish icon of wifely fidelity. However, he also portrays Vittoria's husband, Camillo, as old and foolish, rather than the young

Peretti of fact. He displays no knowledge of the multiple wedding ceremonies of Vittoria and Paolo, and makes the Duke's death the result of poison and strangulation. Curiously, the affection that these two lovers undoubtedly had for each other, even to the point of Vittoria's attempted suicide, is never shown. Above all else, she is portrayed as a woman ruled by lust, whereas in life her tragedy began with ruthless exploitation by both parents and brothers, who arranged her marriage to make their own fortunes. Webster also makes her a Venetian lady, presumably because of the low reputation of the morals of a city with legalized prostitution. As Thomas Coryat remarks in his *Crudities . . .* (1601), "A Venetian courtesan is famoused throughout Christendom." Webster may also have confused her with that famous Venetian courtesan Bianca Capello, who was married to the Duke of Florence, brother-in-law of the historical Bracciano. In two aspects, however, Isabella's renunciation of Paolo and the arraignment of Vittoria, Webster improves on the known sources, making use of his own legal knowledge to compose an unforgettable trial scene. But in general, even Webster's macabre imagination falls short of the now-known facts.

The playwright imposes his own worldview upon these sordid events. The characters exist in a world of appearances, where nothing is as it seems. Good and evil are turned upside down; the whiteness and brightness of Vittoria's beauty are satanic. Faith and mercy are dead, moral anarchy rules, and individual freedom consists in the survival of the fittest in evil. Yet in her personal defiance at her arraignment and the steadfast courage she displays in the face of death, Vittoria demands respect.

Synopsis

The paradoxical title *The White Devil* is usually applied to Vittoria Corombona, the central figure of the play, signifying the brilliance of her beauty and the viciousness of her soul. But it may also refer to Brachiano, if one considers this play the tragedy of a great man destroyed by a woman.[13] The title is also a means of indicating the central theme of the play—appearance is in constant conflict with reality, good and evil are reversed, and humanity attempts to live in a world that accepts the individual as its god. The term *white devil* also appears in a significant proverb: "the white devil is worse than the black," and the term was also applied to hypocrites and nonconformists in general, whether so defined by religious belief or the manner of their lives. But there is also a satanic aspect to the character of Vittoria, in that she is always spoken of as being superb in her brightness, like Lucifer, the angel of light who became the father of lies. Similarly, the play itself contains many references to the diabolical, to darkness, and to death, both physical and spiritual.

"Banisht!"—the opening one-word speech of the decayed Count Lodovico, brings together both the title and the overriding theme of persons operating outside the laws of human behavior. Like Satan, Lodovico has been cast forth from the realm of light, the court, and will henceforth live his life in a world of darkness, vengeance, and crime. It is no accident that his are the last words of the major participants in this tale of bloodshed, lust, and amorality: "I limb'd [*sic*] this night-piece and it was my best" (5.6.297). Lodovico has been exiled for unspecified crimes and while raging against his enemies he notes that Paulo Giordano Orsini, Duke of Brachiano, currently attempting to "prostitute" the honor of Vittoria Corombona, wife to Camillo, has not been punished.

In act 1, scene 2, Vittoria and her brother, Flamineo, the confidant of Brachiano, are briefly introduced. Brachiano's line "Quite lost, Flamineo" (1.2.3), echoes the hopelessness of Lodovico, but in this case, he is lost in lust for Vittoria, whose husband, Camillo, is a foolish older man. Flamineo, acting as pander to his sister, contemptuously tricks Camillo into helping Brachiano to seduce Vittoria. The wicked brother then interprets Vittoria's long, involved dream to suggest that Brachiano should arrange for the murders of Camillo and his own wife, Isabella de Medici. Cornelia, mother of the Corombona brood and the ineffectual moral center of the play, opposes the plan: "What? because we are poor, / Shall we be vicious?" (1.2.314–15).

In act 2 Isabella comes to court with her young son Giovanni Orsini, to enlist the help of Francisco de Medici, Duke of Florence (her elder brother) in regaining her husband's affections. Webster emphasizes Giovanni's love for his mother and the sympathy all her friends and relatives feel for her. When Isabella and Brachiano meet privately he coldly, solemnly, and in legal language, declares himself separated from her. Isabella, though unforgiving toward her rival, Vittoria, reveals herself as virtuous, loving, and unselfish; to save Brachiano's reputation she publicly separates herself from him, before witnesses, using the same formal language to solidify the legality of her act.

Brachiano and Flamineo now arrange the murders of the two unwanted spouses, portrayed on the stage in dumb show. Isabella is the first to die. An accomplice anoints a portrait of Brachiano with deadly poison, and when Isabella follows her nightly ritual of prayers, followed by kissing the picture, she dies. Camillo's neck is broken by Flamineo in a simulated accident on a vaulting horse. Brachiano watches these events with the aid of a magic cap supplied by a conjuror.

Act 3, the high point of the play, portrays the trial of Vittoria as a "debauch'd and diversivolent woman" (3.2.28), an adulteress and murderess, before Cardinal Monticelso (a politic churchman), Duke Francisco, and all the ambassadors of Rome. With insufficient evidence to indict them, Marcello, Vittoria's elder brother, laments his sister's fall from virtue, and Flamineo gives more evidence of his own villainy. Vittoria brilliantly plays the role of innocent, and since the evidence of her complicity in the murder of Camillo is circumstantial, the Cardinal and Francisco emphasize the charges of lust. She responds to all accusations with contempt and will not admit any responsibility for the death of Camillo, refusing to be stigmatized as a whore and strumpet, insisting

> That beauty and gay clothes, a merry heart,
> And a good stomach to a feast, are all,
> All the poor crimes that you can charge me with.
>   (3.2.208–10)

This defiance, coupled with the brilliance of her beauty and skill in deceit, gives her an impressive appearance of innocence before the relentlessly hostile court. Nonetheless she is condemned to residence in "a house of convertites" (3.2.264), while Flamineo and Marcello are released on their own sureties, and Brachiano goes free. Quite rightly, Vittoria claims that this is a "rape" of justice. But then Webster skillfully undercuts her bravura performance by introducing the young Giovanni, mourning for his dead mother, and the audience's sympathy is reversed. Flamineo, fearing discovery of his part in the murders, now feigns madness. He quarrels with Lodovico, who has now been pardoned.

The remainder of the play emphasizes the vengeance of Francisco de Medici, Duke of Florence, and Cardinal Monticelso, who have been unable to agree on a policy toward Brachiano. In act 4 the Cardinal decides to bide his time, but Francisco, following the appearance of Isabella's ghost, chooses to act. First he attempts to sow dissension between the lovers by sending Vittoria a love letter. Flamineo and Brachiano intercept it and the lovers quarrel, but Vittoria (here indeed a victim) convinces Brachiano of her innocence. Reconciled, Brachiano spirits Vittoria from her imprisonment. The news of their flight from Rome coincides with the elevation of Cardinal Monticelso to the papacy, under the name of Paul IV.

The new Pope instantly excommunicates the pair and banishes their followers, while Francisco bribes Lodovico to murder Brachiano. Suspicious of both Francisco and Lodovico, the pontiff learns in confession from the hired assassin of his secret passion for the murdered Isabella and his plan to avenge her death. The Pope refuses absolution to Lodovico, but, tricked by Francisco, Lodovico decides to continue his vengeful course.

In act 5, Brachiano and Vittoria are celebrating their marriage with a tournament in Padua. Seven Moors who are in fact Francisco (disguised as Mulinassar), Lodovico, Antonelli, Gasparo, and three others, similarly disguised arrive to offer service to Brachiano, who greets them warmly, rewards "Mulinassar" for his exploits against the Turks, and invites them to join the celebratory tournament. Flamineo now demonstrates further wickedness as he speaks subversively of Brachiano's generosity, and also reveals his own affair with Zanche, the Moorish maidservant of Vittoria. In a weak moment he promised her marriage, but now does not want to make good on the bargain. Left alone with his younger brother, Marcello, Flamineo insults the honor of their mother, Cornelia, and then kills Marcello in front of Cornelia who goes mad with grief.

Just before the fight at the barriers Francisco and Flamineo initiate Lodovico's plan to sprinkle Brachiano's helmet with perspiration-activated poison. The Duke is carried screaming to his deathbed where he is visited by Lodovico and Gasparo disguised as Capuchins. They parody the ritual of extreme unction but when they are alone with the dying man they reveal themselves, torture him with the certainty of his damnation, and finally strangle him in the presence of his horrified wife. His last words are "Vittoria?/Vittoria!" (5.3.167–68). Now Zanche has fallen in love with the disguised Francisco, and as evidence of her good faith reveals the hitherto unknown circumstances of the murders of Camillo and Isabella, confessing that she herself had a part in them.

Flamineo now tries to regain his former influence at court, but after the burial of Marcello and the shock of Cornelia's madness he experiences an unfamiliar feeling—which, for want of a better term, he calls "compassion." Suddenly Brachiano's ghost appears and prophetically throws earth upon him, signifying his imminent death. Desperately, he rushes to Vittoria's apartment to tell his sister of these events. He will either gain "bounty" from her or kill her.

When he confronts her he tells her that he has decided to die and claims that he has vowed to Brachiano that neither he nor Vittoria should outlive him "The numb'ring of four hours" (5.6.35). Vittoria pleads for her life, but Zanche shrewdly suggests that Flamineo should teach them "The way to death; let him die first" (5.6.74). Flamineo agrees, giving the women four pistols, two to kill him and one for each of them to shoot the other. Although they promise "Most religiously" (5.6.99) to die, they break their word. After shooting at Flamineo they tread on him, and threaten him with the burial customary to suicides—beneath the crossroads with a stake driven through his heart. But Flamineo arises unwounded, because the pistols had held no bullets. He has tested the women and now Lodovico and Gasparo, still disguised as Capuchins, arrive with two other Florentine assistants to dispatch all three.

Vittoria, like her historical counterpart, dies nobly. She refuses to allow Zanche to be killed before her: "I will be waited on in death" (5.6.217). She does not cry, cringe, or beg. Instead she taunts her murderer, Lodovico, accepts the justice of her fate and dies on a sententia:

> O happy they that never saw the court,
> Nor ever knew great man but by report.
> (5.6.261–62)

Zanche has no final line, but Flamineo dies with a certain panache, refusing all funeral ceremonial.

Lodovico and his banditti are not exempt from punishment, and Webster (with a certain amusing chauvinism) brings in the English Ambassador to execute ultimate judgment on the murderers. Lodovico dies as he has lived, by violence, welcoming it, and in effect praising the events of the play as his perfection of the practice of murder as a fine art. The play concludes with the young Giovanni ready to succeed his late father. He seems well prepared to take over this corrupt dukedom, for he delights in warlike pursuits and looks forward to the exercise of rule. He demonstrates a precocious understanding of the ramifications of statecraft.

Critical Comments

The White Devil is an extraordinary play in an age of great tragedies. It is also a most disturbing work in terms of the bleak worldview that it presents; it is as if God has abandoned the world of His creation, leaving humanity to work out its problems unaided. Evil is rampant throughout. Even Cornelia, the moral center of the play, suffers the loss of her children and eventually her sanity. One wonders whether in assigning her this unhistoric name, Webster intended to invite sardonic comparison with the Roman Cornelia, mother of the Gracchi, often praised in courtesy books for her description of her three children ("These are my jewels"). In some ways the echo is apt, for her two sons were both assassinated, but whereas the Gracchi remained united, in *The White Devil* all family ties are presented as tenuous.

Human relationships are perverted by evil and self-interest so that the Corombona family is destroyed by the lust of Vittoria, and the unnatural wickedness, pandering, and fratricide of Flamineo, whose last wish is to murder his own sister. All the marriages of the play are either contracted in lust or destroyed by that deadly sin. Characters believe only in the earthly power of the individual to fulfill viciously selfish desires at any cost. Lodovico is right when he refers to the events of the play as a "night-piece," for the action takes place in interiors where evil deeds are performed in darkness, reinforced by iterated imagery of the charnel house, tombs, death, and decay. Illumination comes from Flamineo, whose name means torch or flame, and from the hard, brilliant, diamond-like reflective brightness of Vittoria. The imagery that surrounds her person emphasizes her ambivalent and seductive wickedness; like a comet she personifies imminent disaster. Her whiteness, then, also indicates the sheer nothingness and blankness of evil, a topic explored by Herman Melville in his section on "The Whiteness of the Whale" in *Moby-Dick*.[14]

All the action revolves about this singular lady, yet her real identity remains elusive. She speaks no soliloquies to reveal the truth of her heart and head, and she falls so easily and skillfully into responsive role-playing that the audience never knows whether she is sincere or playacting. Her brilliant defiance in the trial scene has made even sober critics consider the possibility of her innocence, but the message of Webster's imagery belies her demeanor and supports her guilt. She appears to wish the deaths of both Camillo and Isabella, if one accepts Flamineo's interpretation of her alleged dream (1.2.231–58), but then he, his own sister's pander, is an unreliable witness. Finally, the manner in which she meets her death demands respect, yet even then she knows no real direction: "My soul, like to a ship in a black storm, / Is driven I know not whither" (5.6.248–49).[15] Flamineo likewise offers no answer and takes refuge in sententiae: "We cease to grieve, cease to be Fortune's slaves, / Nay cease to die by dying" (5.6.252–53).

This constantly shifting perspective is the major difficulties of the play. One character acts, speaks, or is acted upon, and another evaluates the situation from his or her personal viewpoint. Scenes undercut each other, operate disjunctively, wrenching the audience's emotions and moral commitments. Each person adopts a stance that is entirely self-generated, caring nothing for the fate of others in the play. Exceptions to this state of being are Cornelia and Marcello, who demonstrate unselfishness and consideration for others. But they are easily destroyed, Marcello by an act of fratricide and Cornelia by the madness that it induces.[16]

"Integrity of life" has been suggested as the central principle of belief and indeed action, for this play and for all of Webster's characters, but it is hard to accept evil as a statement of integrity, even as an aesthetic device.[17] In fact, one cannot fully achieve identification with any of the characters of the play, and quite clearly Webster planned it that way. His vision of what Flamineo calls "this busy trade of life" is unclouded by moral considerations, just like that of his Machiavellian creations. He operates as an unbiased reporter of events for much of the time; as a result, his characters are continually presented with a sardonic detachment as they move through the terrifying motions of their lives in a world devoid of belief or hope of an afterlife.

Yet they do possess an energy in the pursuit of their individualism which defies anything life, or fate, can offer. They glory in their all too human loneliness, exercising a tragic, almost existential freedom which can bring them only to death. But as Cornelia's superb and frequently quoted burial poem shows (5.4.95–104), even the dead are not safe from the wolf, and the permanency of the grave is threatened by the proximity of the charnel house.

The quirky, sardonic, bitter humor of the play, then, may also be seen as proper to proud, independent humanity jesting in confrontation with death. These characters assert their individual freedom to flout conventions in the face of universal corruption, and, as a result, villains like Lodovico and Flamineo take professional delight in their criminal skill, while Brachiano feels no remorse for the death of Isabella. An inconvenience has been removed and his callous comment, "Excellent, then she's dead" (2.2.24), is followed by the professional appraisal of Camillo's demise: " 'Twas quaintly done, but yet each circumstance / I taste not fully" (2.2.38–39). It is in moments like this that Webster reveals character. Such a man as Brachiano has more than an amateur appreciation of brilliant and suitable murders; doubtless his, too, is a practiced hand. Yet when at the end of his life he screams from the pain of his poisoned helmet and then is tortured spiritually by his disguised enemies before being strangled, one suspends judgment on him because he is now the victim. He has dared all for love of Vittoria, and he has temporarily gained his goal; in a sense, his life is a triumph as he dies with her name on his lips. He not only achieved Vittoria, but also a personal victory against the hostility of family, society, and, if only temporarily, even fate itself.

Looked at in this way, Vittoria herself combines victim, female Machiavel, and triumphant woman. Her first marriage made her the victim of social conventions, and she used villainy to remove herself from it, while her second advanced her in rank and possessions, gaining for her the love of a greater man than her impotent, foolish first husband. In changing his source, Webster manages to generate some sympathy for the lovers; the real Vittoria had been married to a young man and her remarriage was to an older and grossly corpulent one, for whom she apparently had some affection. But lest one be too sympathetic, Webster develops satirical echoes through Zanche. She is the black infidel who is the counterpart to Vittoria's whiteness, one who stands outside the moral strictures of a corrupt church, who plots to advance herself in marriage, first with Flamineo, and then with Mulinassar, the disguised Francisco, breaking her oath of silence to a Christian by revealing to a supposed fellow-Moor her complicity in the murders of Camillo and Isabella.

Repetition leads to reinforcement and expansion so that one is forced to consider the possibility that all women are corrupt. This thesis is promptly demonstrated when both Vittoria and Zanche unite to outwit Flamineo, only to find the biter bit. One wonders, then, whether the white devil is really worse than the black? But of all the villains of the play, Flamineo is the ultimate one. The precursor of Bosola in *The Duchess of Malfi,* he is the mover and shaker of the majority of events (as distinct from the actual murders for which Lodovico is mainly responsible). He is a Machiavel. Webster gives him no real motivation— merely a delight in doing evil—and his name signifies the light of wickedness which does not truly illuminate what Milton later called the "darkness visible" of heaven's obverse. But his evil has a purpose— self-aggrandizement—as he pursues advancement through both Brachiano and his own sister. He owes no loyalty to God or man, for he has no ideals, no beliefs. He is a cynic who expects nothing but the worst from all humankind, and he is not disappointed. Like his sister, he is a consummate actor, and his staged "death" is a tour de force of role playing.

Critics have tried, but no one has offered a fully satisfying solution to the actions of the play. Even the ascent of the young Giovanni to the ducal seat of his father should not give rise to universal rejoicing. Certainly he has loved his mother, Isabella, but from his first entrance he has shown himself committed to warfare. To be sure, he censures Flamineo, telling him to do penance, instantly orders the conspirators to prison and torture, and ends the play with a politic platitude. But the apple does not fall far from the tree and one is left with a legitimate doubt whether he, as the product of a corrupt court, will be any better than those he succeeds. Yet at the same time, one wonders whether in drawing this young man, Webster had in mind the Herculean ideal of Henry, Prince of Wales, son of James I, whose almost imminent death the poet was later to celebrate in *A Monumental Column*.[18]

Webster's detachment and ironic worldview should, one thinks, make this play relevant today, but such is not the case. Perhaps audiences are jaded by the familiarity of quotidian violence and see this play more as a series of "special effects" than an attempt to raise serious questions about life and living. In addition, the modern world has lost the gift of language, and finds the sort of bravura performance that this play requires to be aristocratic and old-fashioned. It may be afraid to recognize "the skull beneath the skin,"[19] and therefore chooses to laugh at Webster's obsession with death in an attempt to deny it. To be sure, Webster's own age was one of questioning and of unbelief, but there was a matrix of cultural responses which instantly allowed an audience to recognize as a villain and lost soul any character who trumpeted his total independence in a grand gesture of defiance and selfhood.

In this, his first independent play, Webster's importance is that he is one of the first English playwrights since Shakespeare to give full authentic voice to the moral turmoils of his age and draw characters who attempt to live in the terrifying freedom of what John Donne, Webster's contemporary, calls that "new philosophy [that] calls all in doubt." Thus Webster suddenly and unpredictably emerges as a precursor of those modern playwrights who show the flimsiness of the myths by which much of humanity lives.

Chapter Four
The Duchess of Malfi

By universal acclaim John Webster's greatest work is his next independent tragedy, *The Duchess of Malfi*. Like its predecessor, *The White Devil*, its central character is a woman, but where Vittoria Corombona was a character active in evil, the Duchess is virtuous despite her bold enterprise in defying familial and societal strictures and asserting her freedom of choice. This time there are two wicked brothers, one of whom doubles as a villainous churchman, and the malcontent villainy of Bosola reaches greater heights of dramatic refinement than the earlier Lodovico. Once again Webster portrays a world where evil holds sway, but *The Duchess of Malfi* is even more frightening in its ineffable sadness, because it subverts morality by showing the destruction of what is good. Love, decency, goodness, and repentance are powerless; what survives is the memory of the Duchess's courage and nobility—the virtues of a woman who dared to risk everything for love and had the strength to endure the consequences.

Text

The title page of the First Quarto (1623) reads as follows:

THE / TRAGEDY / OF THE DVTCHESSE / Of Malfy. / *As it was Presented priuately, at the Black- / Friers; and publiquely at the Globe, By the* / Kinges Maiesties Seruants. / The perfect and exact Coppy, with diuerse / *things Printed, that the length of the Play would* / not beare in the Presentment. VVritten by John Webster. / Hora.——*Si quid*—— / ——*Candidus Imperti si non his vtere mecum.*[1] // *LONDON:* / Printed by Nicholas Okes for Iohn / Waterson, and are to be sold at the / signe of the Crowne, in *Paules* / Church-yard, 1623.

The text for this play is good; it was prepared with considerable care for readers, not theatrical performance, something that is corroborated by the paucity of its stage directions. Though proofreading at the press was erratic, errors are few, probably because the compositors had a clean manuscript from which to work. Perhaps Ralph Crane, long associated with the King's Men, was the scrivener, while Webster himself may have made corrections in press since his neighbor, Nicholas Okes, was again the printer.[2]

The printed version is unusual not only because of its length, but also because it is the first English play to preface the text with a complete *Dramatis Personae* listing both the characters and the names of the actors who played them. It also groups the characters actively involved in individual scenes at the beginning of the scene instead of giving them separate entrances. Clearly, the aim was to launch the publication with some fanfare, because it contains a dedication to Baron Berkeley and commendatory verses from the playwrights Thomas Middleton, William Rowley, and John Ford, testifying to the importance of the occasion. Other quarto editions followed in 1640, 1678, and 1707.

Date

Only one thing is certain about the date of *The Duchess of Malfi:* it must have been performed prior to 16 December 1614, when death claimed William Ostler, named in the published cast list as the player of Antonio. Webster must have begun work on his second independent tragedy shortly after the performance of *The White Devil* in early 1612, even though he was also occupied with the publication of that play and the composition of his poetic tribute to the late Prince Henry, who had died in November 1612. Webster's funerary poem, printed in *A Monumental Column* (1613), contains a number of echoes of *The Duchess of Malfi* and also draws on some of the same sources used in the play.[3]

That writing continued throughout 1613 can be inferred from Webster's use of other sources, for instance Sir Philip Sidney's *Arcadia,* reprinted in 1613, and Sir Thomas Overbury's didactic poem, *A Wife.*[4] All this evidence leads one to assign the date of the first performance to the winter of 1613–14 or the spring or autumn of 1614.[5]

Stage History

The participants in the first performance of *The Duchess of Malfi* are known.[6] The King's Men fielded a strong cast: John Lowin played the premier role of Bosola, Richard Burbage, the noted Shakespearean tragic actor, was Ferdinand, and William Ostler acted Antonio.[7] The fact that

the three roles of Ferdinand, the Cardinal, and Antonio are each assigned
to two actors indicates changes made for a revival at an unknown later
date. Information given on the title page suggests that the play was
first performed in the indoor private Blackfriars theater and later
transferred to the open-air public Globe, which had by then been rebuilt
and modernized after its destruction by fire in 1612. In addition, some
of the stage action indicates that the play was designed with an indoor
theater in mind.[8] Certainly night scenes could be simulated by flaming
torches, but "the Masque of Madmen" and the Duchess's inability to
identify Antonio's waxen image both imply the existence of more
sophisticated lighting effects. How these scenes could have been managed
on an open stage in daylight is difficult to conceive, leaving one wondering
whether some of the "diuerse things" included in the printed text might
not include excisions necessitated by the staging limitations endemic to
public theaters.

A curious topical reference in the opening speech of the play, concerning
the French king's reform of his corrupt court, refers to a well-known
murder of 1617. This suggests an interpolation made for a revival
about that time, but records of performances are lacking up to the
closing of the theaters in 1642.[9] After the restoration of the Stuart
monarchy in 1660, *The Duchess of Malfi* was performed in 1662 and
1668, and is listed in the quarto of 1678 as being in the current
repertory of the Duke's Theatre, where it was played with William
Betterton as Bosola and his wife (the former Mary Saunderson) as the
Duchess. Samuel Pepys expressed "admiration" at their performances.
In 1686 it was presented at court.

In 1707 a cut version was played at the Haymarket Theatre under
the title of *The Unfortunate Duchess of Malfy, or the Unnatural Brothers:
a Tragedy,* and in 1735 Lewis Theobald, the Shakespearean editor,[10]
published his adaptation as *The Fatal Secret: A Tragedy.* The title is
a misnomer, for the secret is merely the announcement of the Duchess's
marriage, and this is by no means fatal since the play unexpectedly
ends with the reunion of the couple and their twelve-year-old son after
a series of murders outside the Royal Monument. Theobald, who had
castigated Webster for ignoring the unities of time, place, and action,
attempted to impose them on his predecessor's sprawling play. By
keeping the action entirely in the area of Malfi and beginning the play
after the marriage, he tried to classicize the action, but the unity of
time defeated him. In his efforts to make Webster's horrors palatable
to the eighteenth-century stage he succeeds only in weakening the play.

The scene with the madmen is omitted, a wax image of the Duchess deceives Ferdinand into thinking her dead, and his eventual lycanthropy is broadly hinted at throughout the play. This version was performed at the Theatre-Royal, Covent Garden, where it was *"prais'd and forsaken,"* owing to "political ferment," and has since been deservedly forgotten.[11]

The nineteenth century found Webster's horrors and amorality too much to bear; accordingly an "expurgated and melodramatised" version by R. H. Horne held the stage, becoming a popular vehicle for actresses both in England and America.[12] In 1892 William Poel, the celebrated reviver of Elizabethan plays, adapted and directed the play with the Independent Theatre Company at the Opéra-Comique. The character of Julia was omitted, but "a Dance of Death" was added.

In the twentieth century the play has been frequently performed with a variety of well-known actors in the major roles. Webster's own text is now the preferred one, although directors generally exercise the privilege of cutting it. Celebrated actresses still relish the title role. Notable English performances are those of 1919, 1935, and 1937 (Dublin). In 1945 a landmark performance presented Peggy Ashcroft as the Duchess with Ferdinand played by John Gielgud, the first recorded actor to emphasize the incestuous attraction of brother and sister. The director of this successful production was the celebrated Shakespearean scholar/director George Rylands. Dame Peggy repeated her role in 1960. More recent English productions include an avant-garde production of 1971 by the Royal Court, set in a lunatic asylum, and a traditional one by the Royal Shakespeare Company in the same year, with further traditional productions in 1971, 1976, and 1985; 1985 also saw another avant-garde production.

In the United States, the first recorded performance of the Horne adaptation of *The Duchess of Malfi* took place in San Francisco in 1857. This was followed by touring companies in the same version. Then, in 1946 George Rylands was engaged to repeat his successful London production of the play in New York (38 performances) as a vehicle for Elisabeth Bergner as the Duchess, and the black actor, Canada Lee, as Bosola (playing in white face). Despite the music of Benjamin Britten and an adaptation by W. H. Auden, it was unenthusiastically received.[13] The play has since had many revivals, including 1957 (Phoenix Theatre), 1960 (New York and Ashland, Oregon), 1966 (New York), 1969 (New Haven, Connecticut), 1971 (Stratford, Ontario), and 1976 (Los Angeles).

Two operatic treatments also exist, by Stephen Oliver (performed Oxford, 1971; Santa Fe, New Mexico, 1978) and Stephen Douglas Burton (performed Wolf Trap, Washington, D.C., 1978). The first of these is a spare, modern piece, and the second lush and romantic.[14]

Sources

Webster may not have been aware of it, but the original story of the Duchess of Amalfi, recounted by Matteo Bandello, Bishop of Agen, in part 1, novella 26 of his collected works, had its basis in historical fact. Indeed, Bandello actually may have met Antonio Bologna in Milan, and since the "Delio" of the tale could well be the author himself, Bandello might have been one of those who went to the aid of the murdered man.[15]

The historical Duchess of Amalfi was Giovanna, a granddaughter of the infamous Aragonese King Ferdinand I of Naples. She was married in 1490, at the age of about twelve, to Alfonso Piccolomini, great-nephew of Pope Pius II. Alfonso succeeded his father, Carlo, as Duke of Amalfi in 1493, but died in 1498, leaving his wife pregnant with a son who was born the following year. She ruled the duchy as regent, administering the estates, improving the finances of the family, and remaining unmarried until around 1504 when she met Antonio Bologna, an impoverished member of good family whom she engaged as her major domo.

Soon the two fell in love and were married secretly in an exchange of consents witnessed only by a serving woman, because the Duchess feared her brothers' anger. For some years the marriage was kept secret, but rumors began after the birth of a second child. Antonio, hoping to avoid trouble, left his pregnant wife at home and fled to Ancona in 1510. Using the pretext of a pilgrimage to Loretto, the Duchess followed him to Ancona and there revealed their clandestine marriage to her strangely unsuspecting household. After the birth of a son, the lovers were left in peace for nearly a year, when they were again pursued. Certain that her brothers would not harm her, the Duchess persuaded Antonio to flee with their eldest son, while she remained behind with the two younger children. She was captured, taken to one of her castles, and never seen again.

Antonio meanwhile managed to reach Milan where he lived for over a year, not knowing his wife's fate. Still entertaining the hope of reconciliation with her brothers, he believed (according to Bandello's narrator) that his Duchess would be restored to him. The brothers, however, hired an assassin, who warned Antonio, but in October 1513 Antonio was stabbed to death by a party of four ruffians led by a Lombard captain named Daniel da Bozolo. As told by Bandello the tale is presented in a direct, neutral manner emphasizing the human situation of two lovers destroyed by the powerful and wicked brothers of the Duchess.

This extraordinary tale of love and violence was speedily revised and translated into French by François de Belleforest as the first tale in book 2 of his highly moralized *Histoires Tragiques* (1565). In turn it was translated by William Painter as tale number twenty-three in *The Palace of Pleasure* (1567). As usual, Belleforest augmented and inflated his source to soporific proportions with the addition of soliloquies, classical precedents, interminable sermons, adumbrations and vilifications, adopting throughout a puritanically moral tone that reduces the romantic love of the Duchess for Antonio to an exemplum of lust in which the principals are justly punished. Painter follows suit, suggesting that woman is singularly prone to this deadly sin, and that to some extent the happenings are what might be expected in that religiously benighted country, Italy.

Webster in his turn makes some alterations, most importantly in displaying total sympathy for the Duchess. Bosola becomes the central, ambiguous villain, a complex character who repents his part in the Duchess's murder; the brothers' warnings against remarriage are made to stand as an ominous counterpoint to the wooing scene; the possibility of the Duchess's marriage is discovered after the birth of her first child, not her second; and the reason for Antonio's departure for Ancona (alleged dishonesty) is invented. Also, since Webster has the couple part even before the arrival of the pursuers, Antonio has sometimes been accused of cowardice. The Julia subplot is invented and Castruchio is the lady's husband rather than the name of a cardinal. Finally, in the tortures and the details surrounding the deaths of the Duchess and Cariola, Webster's macabre imagination is fully exploited.

Webster's principal source was Belleforest as translated by Painter. He may also have consulted the French text, even taking a phrase or two from Bandello, though he probably did not read Italian fluently. Additional sources include Giraldi Cinthio's version of the Duchess's tale as translated by George Whetstone in *The Heptameron of Ciuill Discourses* (1582), day five, for the madmen; the *Arcadia* of Sir Philip Sidney (printed 1593, reprinted 1604, 1613), for the imprisonment of

Pamela and Philoclea by Queen Cecropia; Simon Goulart, *Histoires admirables de nostre temps,* translated by Edward Grimeston (1607), for a description of Ferdinand's lycanthropy; together with references to Francesco Guicciardini's *History of Italy,* translated into English by Geoffrey Fenton (1579, reprinted 1599). Echoes of George Chapman's *Seven Penitential Psalms* and John Donne's *Second Anniversary, of the Progress of a Soul* (both 1612) have also been traced.[16] In addition, Webster may have known *El Mayordomo de le Duquesa de Amalfi* by Lope de Vega, though he does not seem to have used it.[17]

Synopsis

The young, widowed Duchess of Malfi falls in love with Antonio Bologna, a penniless man of good family employed as her major domo. Owing to the difference in their rank, the Duchess is forced to woo for herself, and they celebrate their marriage secretly. Consents are exchanged in words of the present tense, *per verba de praesenti,* in the presence of Cariola, the Duchess's serving maid.[18]

Privacy and secrecy are essential because the Duchess's two brothers, Ferdinand, her twin, and the Cardinal, the oldest member of the family, forbid her to remarry and force her to swear to follow their wishes. The Duchess readily agrees, having already joined herself in a valid (but unlawful) union with Antonio. The brothers allegedly support the conservative stance of Saint Paul, who advises a widow to devote herself to her husband's memory and her children. But later Ferdinand announces that he and the Cardinal wish the family to retain control of the Malfi money, and even more important, Ferdinand gradually reveals an incestuous passion for his sister.

The Duchess and Antonio manage to keep their relationship secret for several years, in spite of the relentless spying of Daniel de Bosola, a hired villain-malcontent, whom the brothers intrude into the Malfi household. They almost discover her marriage when the suspicious Bosola gives the Duchess apricots to induce premature labor. Bosola even discovers the horoscope Antonio has cast for his son, but remains unaware of the father's identity. The marriage remains secret even after a second child is born, but with the Duchess pregnant for a third time the truth is revealed. In the extraordinary mirror scene (3.2.58–101) the Duchess believes herself to be talking to Antonio, but Ferdinand enters and learns of her remarriage. Still she resourcefully withholds her husband's name. Ferdinand departs in a fury for Rome to inform the

Cardinal and the Duchess arranges for Antonio's flight, concocting an accusation of peculation to account for his "banishment." But then, disarmed by Bosola's praise of Antonio, she reveals his name, information that the spy immediately passes on to the hostile brothers. For the Duchess, Bosola suggests a feigned pilgrimage to Loretto to meet her husband.

Meanwhile the Cardinal is about to go to war as a soldier, and comes to Loretto formally to resign his ecclesiastical office and to be invested as a knight. In dumb-show he performs another ceremony, the banishment of Antonio, the Duchess, and their children. When Bosola arrives with an ambiguous safe conduct from Ferdinand, the Duchess perceives her brother's hostile intent, and suspecting an ambush, counsels Antonio to flee to Milan with his eldest son. No sooner does he ride away than the disguised Bosola, with an armed company, takes the Duchess as a prisoner to her own palace.

Act 4 presents the passion and death of the Duchess. She impresses even Bosola with her nobility in bearing misfortune, but her courage so enrages Ferdinand that he devises a series of grotesque tortures to break her spirit, increasing their torment by inflicting them in the guise of reconciliation and pardon. Finally she is strangled by Bosola. Believing her husband and son to be dead, she greets death with dignity and resignation:

> Pull, and pull strongly, for your able strength
> Must pull down heaven upon me:—
> Yet stay; heaven-gates are not so highly arch'd
> As princes' palaces, they that enter there
> Must go upon their knees.—
>
> (4.2.230–34)

Bosola feels such pity at the sight of the dying woman that he comforts her with assurances that Antonio and their oldest boy live. In stark contrast, Cariola, her serving maid, departs, terror-stricken, to be strangled offstage along with the two youngest children. Such is the Duchess's virtue that it survives her death, causing even Ferdinand to experience an excess of remorse and terror that leads him into lycanthropy.

Haunted by the visions generated by his guilty conscience, the Cardinal now fears discovery, and having revealed the circumstances of his sister's death to Julia, his mistress, he murders her by having her kiss a poisoned Bible.[19] He deputes Bosola to remove her body, but the villain has been so touched by the Duchess's fate that he plans to take vengeance on the brothers and save Antonio. Ironically, Bosola stabs Antonio in a case of mistaken identity. Bosola now repeats his act of charity toward the Duchess, this time informing the dying man that his wife and children are already dead, thereby offering him consolation in the afterlife. Enraged by this accident, Bosola now stabs the Cardinal. Suddenly, the raving Ferdinand bursts in, stabs the Cardinal again and delivers a fatal wound to Bosola who in turn kills Ferdinand. The sole survivor of this unhappy family, Antonio's son, is led in by Delio, his father's confidant, and the play ends on a *sententia: "Integrity of life is fame's best friend, / Which nobly, beyond death, shall crown the end."*

Critical Comments

"Sex, violence and religion" make for dramatic as well as operatic success,[20] and while *The Duchess of Malfi* has all three, it is chiefly memorable for its emphasis on the emotions. Lewis Theobald, in the introduction to his adaptation, *The Fatal Secret* (1735), remarked that he "found something singularly engaging in the Passions, a mixture of the Masculine and the Tender,"[21] which impelled him to modernize it for the taste of the time. And later critics, while generally admiring the strength and endurance of a woman who had the courage to follow her heart and maintain her virtuous "integrity of life" to the end, find themselves profoundly saddened by her fate.

The Duchess is, of course, the central figure, first as initiator of the events, then as their victim, and finally, after her murder, when her spirit pervades the concluding actions of the play. Webster has often been praised for his daring innovation in killing a principal character mid-play, as Shakespeare had earlier done with Julius Caesar, but he is less successful than his master. The fact remains that the last act is anticlimactic, dominated by random violence and a splintering of focus, made even more notable because of its juxtaposition to the preceding act with its single emphasis on the suffering and death of the Duchess. As in *The White Devil*, the plethora of corpses onstage at the finale now tends to evoke laughter. Perhaps this carnage was not comic to Jacobean playgoers, but today the continual escalation of repeated murder anaesthetizes horror and leads to mirth as a form of release.

In this play Webster tries to amalgamate a series of different dramatic forms and influences into a new and original artifact. He may even have taken the masque form and developed it "into a new drama of insecurity and scepticism."[22] Perhaps, as Bradbrook suggests, a fable for *The Duchess of Malfi* might well be "a masque of Good Fame."[23] Thus Bosola would become the masquemaker when he arranges for the dead hand, the waxwork figures, and the dance of madmen as a kind of antimasque before the Duchess. A ritual resonance may also come from the *charivari,* a French mock entertainment given to a woman who remarried immediately after the death of her husband. In other words, Bosola, in presenting this ironic "entertainment" to the Duchess, is signifying the disapproval and distaste felt by the brothers (and initially himself) at the Duchess's conduct.[24] It is, therefore, a parody of the masque of matrimony, and Bosola's dirge, "Hark, now every thing is still" (4.2.178–95), thus becomes an inversion of the epithalamium, a hymn on the occasion of marriage. Similarly, as the revenge tragedy genre frequently concluded with a masque in which the masquers turned on the members of the play/audience and destroyed them, so here the characters destroy each other. At the end, Delio alone remains of their troubled generation, and in introducing Antonio's young son he may signify that once more the universe has returned to rational order.

But that statement begs the question, because the universe portrayed in *The Duchess of Malfi* is by no means rational. Instead, it is perverse and capricious, as Bosola realizes when he inadvertently stabs Antonio, the one man he had hoped to save: "We are merely the stars' tennisballs, struck and banded / Which way please them" (5.4.54–55). The dying man in turn perceives life as ephemeral emptiness:

> In all our quest of greatness,
> Like wanton boys whose pastime is their care,
> We follow after bubbles, blown in th'air.
> Pleasure of life, what is't? only the good hours
> Of an ague; merely a preparative to rest,
> To endure vexation.
>
> (5.4.64–69)

The good and the innocent perish just as violently as the wicked, and the system of rewards and punishments seems irrelevant. In short, justice is not done to all, and the good instincts of the erstwhile villain, Bosola, are thwarted by that unknown force later called by Thomas Hardy "The President of the Immortals."

Of course it is possible to say that *The Duchess of Malfi* is a dramatized treatise upon the consequences of lust, but that is as oversimplified as suggesting that Shakespeare's *Othello* should be read as "a warning to young women to look well to their linen," as Thomas Rymer (1693) said quite seriously.[25] Certainly the role of widows was debated, and that Webster knew of these competing claims is clear from the diametrically opposed characters he wrote for the 1615 edition of the *Characters* of Sir Thomas Overbury: *A vertuous Widdow* eschews remarriage out of respect for her husband's memory, while *An ordinarie Widdow* remarries quickly and often.

Webster's treatment of the Duchess, however, is not morally judgmental. He portrays her as aware and intelligent, understanding the pitfalls that lie ahead of her, sensual in an affirmative sense as a representative of feminine procreative sexuality, proud, and strong-willed. As a noblewoman she is accustomed to ruling a great house and is determined to gain her heart's desire, no matter what the cost. More resourceful than Antonio, she devises stratagems to put her brothers off the scent, publicly accusing Antonio of peculation in order to save his life, and willingly giving herself into the custody of her brothers' minions so that her husband and their oldest child may go free. She is also maternal, and her last words are ones of tender practicality—statements of normalcy in an insane world (4.2.203–5).

In act 4 she grows into spiritual greatness, as she loses all the trappings of temporal power and riches. She never grovels, never questions the rightness of her love; despite marrying her inferior in rank, she still has the pride of her own great birth—"I am Duchess of Malfi still" (4.2.142), she says with her stubborn dignity and selfhood intact.[26] Her nobility and endurance impress even the crime-hardened Bosola, as Ferdinand pushes him into escalating the exquisite mental torture they inflict on her. Like Vittoria Corombona before her, the Duchess meets death boldly, but differs in departing from life certain of salvation, while her predecessor had no such confidence; she died in a mist and with death she passed into uncertainty. The true grandeur of the Duchess's last living gesture is highlighted through its contrast with the screaming fear of Cariola as she is hustled into death while the Duchess welcomes it. Once again Webster has daringly made the central figure of a tragedy a woman, one who has flouted both custom and family, but in this case he has also created a flesh-and-blood character who evokes pathos as well as demands respect. Images of light constantly surround her, dazzling her enemies; unlike Vittoria in *The White Devil*, the Duchess is that pure salvific light that "shineth in the darkness and the darkness comprehended it not" (1 John 1:5). But this light cannot save those she loves, or defend her from those who hate her. In the capricious world of court and corruption she inhabits, innocence is destroyed and repentance is not rewarded.

The unholy trinity consisting of the Duchess's three male enemies is skillfully differentiated. Even the Cardinal, though to some extent the stereotype of the wicked and ambitious Italianate churchman, possesses recognizable personal traits. Like his sister, he is proud and resourceful, but in him these characteristics are exaggerated into vices. Her procreative sexuality becomes lust in him; while he indulges himself with Julia, he hypocritically gives her moral lectures. In his public life he combines both the cross and sword, and is implacable in his pursuit of vengeance. However, he can still feel the terrors of guilt, and the image of the punitive figure in the fishpond (5.5.4–7) is evidence that he still owns a conscience, even though he feels no guilt for Julia's death and has no intention of ceasing his murderous pursuits (since he plans the murders of both Antonio and Bosola). What he really fears is discovery, and in that terror he wades ever deeper into blood.

Ferdinand, however, is a very different case, and in this century more attention has been paid to him because of his suppressed incestuous attraction to his sister. This hidden motivation is important; although Ferdinand is never shown as a lecher like the Cardinal, his language is full of sexuality, and his mind exudes an aura of prurience. Perhaps the true reason for his wish to keep the Duchess unmarried is the result of incestuous desire, but one should also recall the psychic complementarity that exists between twins, even those of different sexes. For Ferdinand, then, his sister represents an unattainable feminine counterpart, as he unconsciously lusts after her and no other woman. Thus, in his psychological frustration, he wishes to keep her "pure," reaching heights of vengeful fury when he discovers her "loose i'th'hilts" (2.5.3). Even more revealing is the way in which he imaginatively recreates the details of that "shameful sin" that dishonors him.[27]

Unstable from the beginning of the play, his final lycanthropic frenzies develop logically from the consequences of his unfulfilled incestuous desire and murderous vengeance on his twin. Yet though he is implacable in his tortures, he is not without a sense of pain. When he perceives the result of his hostility to the Duchess, he is shocked at the sight of the virtue he has destroyed. Forced into the realization that he has killed an irreplaceable part of himself, he delivers Webster's most famous line: "Cover her face: mine eyes dazzle: she died young" (4.2.264). At that moment he reveals their twinship and feels both guilt and loss. Lacking the political acumen and cold logic of his brother, he cannot face what he has done and succumbs to mental disease.

Bosola, the murderous malcontent, is the most interesting male character of the play. Intelligent, cold, calculating, cruel, self-seeking, ironically witty and detached, he nonetheless grows into pity because of his admiration for the virtue of the Duchess. He is the role-player, the chameleon, predictable only in evil. Much has been claimed for his repentance, but in fact he has changed little. The Duchess's influence does not turn him away from a life of violence and her virtue evokes more murderous behavior from this professional killer. To be sure, he does wish to save Antonio and performs an act of mercy toward the dying man in telling him of his wife's death, but forgiveness for evil actions remains foreign to him. The Christian resignation of the Duchess is beyond his moral capacity which even pity has not advanced beyond implacable revenge. He feels some guilt for his actions against the Duchess, but is able to slough it off by blaming his evil deeds on her bloody brothers. However, the sheer energy of his portrayal makes him remarkable.

In comparison, Antonio suffers from his passivity and gentle virtue.[28] He feels affection for the Duchess, and Webster gives him some of the very human attributes of an ambitious servant, but he is reluctant to act for himself. Instead he responds to the Duchess's wooing, and throughout the entire play she is by far the more enterprising of the two. Only in his reactions to the initial threat of discovery, after the Duchess's premature labor, does he show true initiative, but even then he is so distraught by the turn of events that he inadvertently drops the child's horoscope. In addition, his willing acquiescence in riding off with his son, leaving his wife to the untender mercies of her brothers, has often been described as an act of cowardice. One must recall, however, that it was dictated by the source, and further, that Bosola has appeared to be a friend to the lovers. His greatest faults arise from his essential innocence and trust in personal virtue. Afflicted with decency, he cannot suspect the depths of human depravity within the Malfi brothers and hence is able to entertain hopes of reconciliation when the logic of past behavior would suggest otherwise. Further, Webster has not developed his character so as to gain the unqualified sympathy of the audience, because he does not give him any scenes of suffering comparable to those of the Duchess. The echo-scene (5:3) offers foreboding, but does not evoke pity or terror. In short, Antonio suffers by comparison with the energies of evil demonstrated elsewhere in the action. His entire life seems to be the product of hostile accident, and his death at the hand of the man who wishes to save him shows again the capricious nature of that first principle, the primum mobile that governs the happenings of this remarkable play.

The final impression left with the audience is one of profound sadness at the totality of destruction, where virtue is destroyed and incipient repentance cut off before it has the chance to develop. Apparent order is restored at the end of the action, but one fears that the respite is but brief and the darkness of evil will again cover the earth. The life and death of the Duchess offer only a short interlude of virtue in "a naughty world."

Webster apparently followed this triumphant tragedy with a lost play entitled *The Guise* (1614–15), which Forker suggests "may well be the most regrettable of all the lost plays in his canon."[29] Presumably it dealt with the events in France on Christmas Day, 1588, when the third Duc de Guise was assassinated through the machinations of the ineffectual King Henry III of France, son of Catherine de Medici, in order to consolidate his power. Webster's dark genius was well-suited to a portrayal of the plethora of murders resulting from this act, including assassination of the guilty king himself, combined with political plot and counterplot, intrigue, sex, and revenge. Perhaps he was influenced by Christopher Marlowe's *The Massacre at Paris* in his choice of this topic, but even here one cannot be sure, since Webster had earlier used references to the French historian, Pierre Matthieu (who recounts these deeds) in his elegy on Prince Henry, *A Monumental Column*. One can only speculate on the way in which Webster, now in total control of his medium, might have portrayed these events, refracted though his unique vision of darkness and corruption, redeemable only in the nobility of death.

Chapter Five
The Devil's Law-Case

The Devil's Law-Case, the third and last of Webster's independently written plays, has not enjoyed the good reputation of its predecessors, largely because of the complicated plot and mixed dramatic tone that continually keep the audience spinning between the emotional commitment of near-tragedy and the moral detachment evoked by its curious mode of comedy. Unsentimental, "modish" (to quote Forker), indeed hardheaded, this tragicomedy also boasts a conclusion in which the final pairings of characters appear both capricious and confusing although a curious kind of rough justice is served. Also, imprecise stage directions force directors and actors to make performance choices in order to clarify the ending.

Certainly Webster put his heart into this sardonic tragicomedy: the care with which he developed his legal references, and the poetic power of his unexpectedly lyrical passages on the transitory nature of human life indicate his commitment. It also marks a turning point in his dramatic career. As a synthesis of past concerns and an experimental foreshadowing,[1] it is by no means an unworthy successor to the two great independent tragedies.[2]

Text

The title page of the first quarto (1623) reads as follows:

The Deuils Law-case. / OR, / When Women goe to Law, the / Deuill is full of Businesse. / *A new Tragecomœdy.* / *The true and perfect Copie from the Originall.* / As it was approouedly well Acted / by her Maiesties Seruants. / *Written* by IOHN WEBSTER. / *Non quam diu, sed quam bene.* /[3] [Ornament] / LONDON, / Printed by A[ugustine]. M[atthews]. for *Iohn Grismand,* and are / to be sold at his Shop in Pauls Alley at the Signe of the Gunne. 1623.

This quarto is the only seventeenth-century text. In its corrected form it is clean with few problems of compositorial or machine error, although it was extensively corrected during the press run. The basic textual problem concerns the distinction between verse and prose, largely the result of Webster's habit of using varied line lengths, which a recent editor suggests is aimed at approximating everyday speech.[4] Further, since scene divisions are lacking in the quarto, those in all later editions lack authorial imprimatur, although the decisions of F. L. Lucas (1928) are generally accepted. The exact nature of the copy-text remains uncertain, but it may have been authorial.[5] As was apparently his practice, Webster either assisted in the printing process or approved of the finished product and exercised editorial oversight.

This hypothesis is corroborated by the playwright's address "To the Judicious Reader," in which he claims that he, personally, had refused unsolicited offers of commendatory verses. Then, with typical generosity, he writes of the artistic interdependence of actor and playwright: "yet can no action ever be gracious, where the decency of the language, and ingenious structure of the scene, arrive not to make up a perfect harmony." However, he still feels misunderstood, for he concludes with a quotation from Horace: *"Non ego ventosae plebis suffragia venor"* [I am not one to hunt the votes of a fickle public],[6] knowing only too well from the hostile reception of *The White Devil* by "ignorant asses" that "the breath of the uncapable multitude, is able to poison it."[7] The brief prose dedication was written to Sir Thomas Finch, the future Earl of Winchilsea, whom the playwright had not met but who had seen *The White Devil, The Duchess of Malfi* and *The Guise,* but whether in print or in performance is unknown.

Date

The date 1623 on the quarto title page is clearly not the date of composition, and there is no hard evidence to aid the scholar. One detail, the reference in the dedication to the lost play *The Guise,* offers some help since it probably followed the two major tragedies. This would place *The Devil's Law-Case* between 1613 and 1623. Further corroboration can be found in the title page reference to its having been "Acted / by her Maiesties Seruants." Queen Anne, wife of King James I, died in 1619, and while the company may have continued to use the old matronal name for a while, it is unlikely that the practice would have extended as late as 1623. Further, since the title page notes the play as "new," one would expect that publication followed performance with reasonable speed.

Internal evidence offers a fertile field for speculation. For instance, the numbers given in the trial scene (4.2), which establish Romelio's age, add up to 1610, a date which has not been generally accepted. Similarly, Winifrid's reference to "two great frosts" (4.2.433) would place the play after the frosts of 1564 and 1607–8, and before the one of 1621. Other hints may come from an incident in the Dutch East Indies of October 1619 (4.2.11–14), and a currency smuggling case of 1619, while a famous incest trial of 1619–20 had incited pulpit blasts against "the insolence and impudence of Women."[8]

But the formal Jacobean controversy over women had been in full swing since the 1615 publication of *The Arraignment of Lewde, idle, froward, and vnconstant women: or the vanitie of them, choose you whether* by Joseph Swetnam. This book called forth many rejoinders, including an anonymous play titled *Swetnam the Woman-hater Arraigned by Women*.[9] What is noteworthy is the arraignment situation that Webster may well have been exploiting through the resurrection of popular antifeminism in this play.

Thus a date of somewhere around 1619–20 for completion of the play appears most likely. Judging from Webster's recorded work habits, the period of 1617 to early 1621 seems to establish suitable parameters for its composition, though Forker suggests a performance date of 1617 or 1618.[10] In other words, no real consensus exists.

Sources

This play is unique in Webster's canon because no single source has been found and the plot may well be original with the playwright, something unusual for this transmutational genius.[11] Nonetheless, there are numerous parallels for specific parts of this complex play.

The incident of the attempted murder that becomes a lifesaving operation probably comes from Simon Goulart, *Histoires admirables de nostre temps,* translated by Edward Grimeston (1607), the same source from which Webster took the lycanthropy of Ferdinand in *The Duchess of Malfi.* Leonora's attempted bastardizing of her son also appears elsewhere, most notably in the anonymous play *Lust's Dominion, or the Lascivious Queen,* attributed to John Day, William Haughton, and Thomas Dekker (ca. 1600, published 1657), and later in *The Fair Maid of the Inn* (ca. 1625–26, published 1647), probably in part by Webster. But behind both these plays is apparently a popular tale that involves an attack by a mother on her son's legitimacy. Because specific details differ in individual treatments and analogues, the exact amount of indebtedness is impossible to determine.[12] In addition, Webster also borrowed from other dramas, including *Sejanus* by Ben Jonson and *The Malcontent* by John Marston. In the latter case he was in a sense borrowing from himself, since he had collaborated with Marston in a revision of that work.

Stage History

There is no record of the play's performance except for the comment on the title page that "it was approouedly well Acted / by her Maiesties Seruants." Thus the first performance was probably at the genteel Cockpit/Phoenix theater.[13] There are no recorded revivals until the Theatre Royal production at York, England, in 1980, when Michael Winter directed it to mixed reviews. No professional productions have been recorded in the United States. Thus, the play has essentially no theater history. This is a pity, because there are some extremely good scenes, particularly that of the trial (4.2), which should still prove capable of holding the stage. However, a modern audience might prove unfriendly to the antifeminism of the plot and the uncertainty of tone and emotional commitment evident throughout. Yet *The Devil's Law-Case* remains disturbingly relevant because it portrays a world regrettably similar to our own in its commercialism and pursuit of self-interest.

Synopsis

In Naples, Romelio, called "The Fortunate Young Man" but really an unscrupulously successful merchant, is interrupted in his boasting by the young lord Contarino, who wishes to sell Romelio some of his inherited land to pay his gambling debts. Contarino then announces his desire to wed Jolenta, the merchant's sister, revealing that they are already vowed to each other and need only the consent of Romelio and his mother, Leonora.

Contarino, not quite trusting Romelio, whose "innocent vainglory" he notes, now tries to gain the consent of Leonora, but first he plans to discover whether his future mother-in-law approves of him. Consequently, he engages the older woman in courtly badinage, and to his surprise is offered forty thousand crowns from her own coffers so that he can retain his patrimony. Not realizing that she is in love with him, he jumps to the convoluted conclusion that Leonora has already discovered

his intentions toward Jolenta. His confusion is compounded by a letter
from his beloved warning him of danger.

Romelio now presents Jolenta with Ercole, a knight of Malta, a
candidate for her hand approved by the King of Spain, but the astonished
Jolenta refuses him, standing firm against her brother's wishes. Ercole,
angrily accusing Romelio of deceiving him, threatens to demand retri-
bution for his humiliation. The merchant attempts to placate Ercole
and taxes Jolenta with wishing to marry Contarino.

Leonora also opposes Jolenta's marriage to the gambler, Contarino.
Dissembling, she announces that she herself has decided never to remarry
and presses the cause of Ercole, insisting on an immediate marriage
contract. Despite her protestations, the weeping Jolenta is forced to go
through a ceremony of espousal in which her reluctance is deliberately
misconstrued as virtuous modesty. After Ercole's departure, Jolenta
berates herself for having submitted to force, telling Contarino that she
will commit suicide rather than marry Ercole. At this, Contarino suggests
immediate marriage, and Jolenta agrees on condition that no harm come
to Ercole.

In act 2, several different aspects of the complex plot are concurrently
developed. Crispiano, Corregidor of Seville, a rich elderly lawyer, comes
in merchant's disguise to Naples to spy upon his son, the spendthrift
Julio, who believes his father dead. He also brings bad news to Romelio
concerning his maritime enterprises. Ariosto, an honest lawyer, attempts
to console and counsel him, but the young man will not accept the
proffered advice.

Contarino now challenges Ercole to a duel over Jolenta and in the
ensuing conflict each deals the other an apparently mortal wound. News
of their "deaths" is brought to Leonora, who is appalled to learn that
they are also to be denied Christian burial. Romelio expresses pity for
Jolenta, who has now lost two matrimonial chances, and then indicates
an unsuspected side to his mercantile personality as he delivers an
eloquent (and typically Websterian) meditation on the vanity of human
life, the evanescence of riches, and the impermanence of the tomb:

> How then can any monument say,
> Here rest my bones till the last day,
> When time swift both of foot and feather,
> May bear them the sexton kens not whither.
> (2.3.137–40)

Immediately afterward, Romelio is informed that Contarino is in fact still alive and has willed all his property to Jolenta. He is chagrined, but Leonora rejoices because he can now suffer "public justice" for having killed Ercole, and offers to send a relic to aid in his recovery. Romelio is suspicious of his mother's mixed signals and excessive interest in Contarino's cure. In the next scene (2.4) Ercole is also discovered to be alive, but the noble gentleman generously wishes that the report of his death be confirmed so that Contarino may wed Jolenta.

Further reasons for the visit of Don Crispiano to Naples are revealed. The King of Spain suspects Romelio of misappropriating funds from a gold mine in the West Indies. But even more important is Crispiano's charge to prevent the "mad tricks" that women have lately played in manipulating their sick husbands into willing them their entire estates. Both the honest lawyers, Ariosto and Crispiano, agree that these practices must be stopped, and Crispiano swears to devote his legal expertise to curbing "the insolencies / Of these women" (3.1.29–30).

After offering to reward the two attending surgeons if they will later aid him in smothering their defenseless patient, Romelio gains entrance to the sickroom of Contarino, ostensibly to persuade the dying man to revise his will. He then stabs him (allegedly to save him from the scaffold, but actually to prevent his marriage to Jolenta). Caught in the act, Romelio reveals his identity to the surgeons who promptly blackmail him. However, his dagger has opened up Contarino's wound. Ironically, Romelio has wrought a cure.

Ignorant of this development, Romelio goes to Jolenta, who is mourning the loss of Contarino. He tells her that she is now Contarino's heir and concocts a plan whereby she will also inherit the land of the Lord Ercole. He suggests that she pretend to be with child by Ercole and when the time of her "delivery" comes, he will substitute the child of his mistress, the pregnant nun, Angiolella. The "precontract" of marriage made between Jolenta and Ercole will justify the situation. Shocked, Jolenta tells him that she is already with child by Contarino. Romelio now suggests that Jolenta's child "be reputed Ercole's," and after her delivery the news be spread abroad that she has produced twins. In this way Ercole's property will come to the family, and Romelio's bastard will receive financial support. Jolenta then reveals that she is not in fact pregnant; she had said so in the hope that her brother would kill her. Romelio now alleges that Leonora and Contarino had planned a ménage à trois had Jolenta married Contarino. Totally appalled, Jolenta now agrees to Romelio's proposition.

Flushed with success, Romelio plans to dispose of his two blackmailing surgeons and then informs Leonora of Jolenta's alleged pregnancy. Leonora thinks only of Contarino, and when Romelio announces that he has murdered him, she delivers a hysterical speech of mourning for this last love of her widowed heart, threatening vengeance on her son (3.3.257–302). As she lies fainting, she is revived by a monk, bringing news of the restoration to life of a dead friend. At first she thinks of Contarino, but when Ercole reveals himself she tells him that Jolenta is carrying his child. Ercole, knowing this to be untrue, but believing the child to be Contarino's, gallantly volunteers to marry the girl. Left alone with her maid, Winifrid, Leonora exchanges confidences with her and crowns forty years of trust by confiding her decision to disgrace and disinherit her son in open court. She asks Winifrid to bring her a picture, whose significance will only become clear in the courtroom scene (4.2).

In act 4 Leonora, accompanied by Winifrid and the clerk Sanitonella, goes to the office of Ariosto, an honest lawyer, to engage his help in her lawsuit. He refuses the case, but Contilupo, "a spruce [crooked] lawyer," is happy to take it. As the trial takes place, with Crispiano as judge, the principals gather, some in disguise. The case mystifies Romelio, who to his astonishment discovers himself at the center of a disinheritance suit, Leonora claiming that he is the illegitimate son of one Don Crispiano. He therefore has no right to his landed inheritance, while Jolenta (though truly begotten) must lose her dower because of her immorality.

The judge then calls Winifrid to give her testimony, which she does with tantalizing detail, but is tripped up on dates. He claims to have been an acquaintance of this same Crispiano and recalls that the gentleman had left his picture with his lady. Anxious now to prove her nonexistent dishonor, Leonora offers to send for the portrait. Then, after ordering it to be hung in open court, Crispiano removes himself from the case as an interested party, turning the bench over to the honest lawyer, Ariosto, and proclaiming his support of Romelio. As his first act, Crispiano bids the entire assemblage look upon the picture and Leonora recognizes him as the man she has accused, while Julio realizes that his father lives. Leonora's trick has failed and she is proved an honest woman, but both she and Winifrid have given false evidence. The serving woman attempts to allege coercion, while Leonora blames Contarino and to save her skin announces that she is about to enter into religion.

All this astounds Contarino who is about to unmask, but Ercole precedes him and is instantly arrested for the dueling death of Contarino. However, Ercole now challenges Romelio over the murder of Contarino, citing his nefarious attempts to procure Contarino's estate for his sister (Ercole has gained this information from Leonora in her distress over Contarino's "death"). The disguised Contarino now realizes the "violence of this woman's love" to him and thinks he understands the motivation for her lawsuit. Ariosto, sitting as judge, finally decrees a duel for the following day between Ercole and Romelio (with the disguised Contarino and Julio as seconds).

The final act begins with a curious dialogue between Jolenta and Angiolella. Jolenta (no longer pretending pregnancy) is flippant in the face of the nun's profound sorrow and shame, but the two women decide to depart together, after leaving a letter for Ercole. In it Jolenta (for some obscure reason) riddles that "the shame she goes withal" was begotten by her brother. This accusation shocks the noble Ercole, who had been prepared to shelter her if her "child" had been Contarino's. Both prospective bridegrooms take her statement literally, thinking of incest, and Contarino says he will think no longer of "her," but he means Leonora. Winifrid, in the meantime, has garnered a proposal of marriage from one of the surgeons who reveals the fact that Contarino lives.

Romelio, presenting a bold facade before the coming duel, is confessed by a Capuchin who knows that Contarino is alive. He tries to get the young man to meditate on death and admit his role in the "murder" of Contarino, but when he refuses the Capuchin does not reveal the truth. Leonora, however, is so sure that the duel will end tragically for her son and his second that she brings in two coffins and winding sheets in preparation for their burial. This stimulates Romelio to express fear of death and he delivers another, even more eloquent peroration on the transitory nature of human existence (5.4.126–47). But then, perhaps reacting to the bravado of his second, Julio, he locks both Leonora and the Capuchin into a closet, telling Julio that he wants to be rid of his mother's "howling." She and the monk, however, wish to save his life, but Romelio misinterprets their shouts.

Just as the combat is about to begin, Romelio has a change of heart and sends for the Capuchin to shrive him. He arrives with Leonora to stop the duel and reveal the identity of Contarino, much to the joy of Ercole, who now vows him eternal friendship. Leonora promptly presses her claims to Contarino, who willingly accepts her. Angiolella and Jolenta (for some reason disguised as a Moor) now return, and upon their identities being revealed, Ariosto pronounces sentence. Romelio must forgive the interest on Julio's debts to him and then marry Angiolella. Contarino, Romelio, and Julio must maintain a galley against the Turk for the next seven years. Leonora, Jolenta and Angiolella must build a monastery in reparation, and the two surgeons who concealed Contarino's escape from death are given one year in the galleys. At some unspecified point, Jolenta is paired off with the faithful Ercole. Angiolella delivers a speech of moral rectitude and thus the order of dramatic expediency is wrought on this extraordinarily puzzling and convoluted play.

Critical Comments

"Uncertainties of response" characterize one's reactions to *The Devil's Law-Case*. For this reason, the convoluted structure of the play, particularly its careful alternation of scenes, must be noted, because of the swiftly shifting juxtaposition of attitudes, themes, and characters.[14] In no other play by Webster is his disjunctive technique so marked, where duplicities abound and sympathies are altered so that the audience remains in a constantly unpredictable state of bemused puzzlement. "Nothing is but what is not."

In this, his last independent play, Webster does not have the luxury of an existing source to keep his muse under control. As a result, in *The Devil's Law-Case* the events take on a life of their own, developing into unexpected patterns, piling one complication on another, in defiance of the logic of life. Psychological motivation is nonexistent and verisimilitude is ignored. The emphasis of the play is on action rather than character, yet it continually displays echoes of and relationships to Webster's earlier and greater tragedies.

The very title of *The Devil's Law-Case* immediately recalls *The White Devil*, and the same dislocation of attitude obtains in the characterization of Leonora and Vittoria. These two women are similar in their independence and insistence on choosing husbands for themselves. But immediately a moral judgment intrudes. Are they perhaps gratifying their own lust, and is this why Webster refers to them both as devils?[15] Certainly they are manipulators, and while one can argue that Vittoria is to some extent the victim of her family's ambition, as well as her own lust, Leonora forfeits sympathy by her perversion of maternal love. She remains a puzzling character, particularly in her willingness to announce herself an adulteress, bastardizing her son in order to gain revenge on him for the killing of a hoped-for lover. It is her last sexual excursion before old age. Yet she also indicates maternal affection by sadly supplying coffins and winding sheets for both Romelio and his second in the impending duel. Then, on learning that Contarino lives, she reverses herself and is equally as determined to save her son from the possibly fatal duel as she was to disinherit him.

Perhaps the true deviltry of Leonora is that she attempts to follow her own desires at any cost, violating decorum in lust, plotting against her own children, and demonstrating that the keynote of her being is self-centered exploitation. One would then expect that she, like Vittoria, should be made to pay dearly, but instead she is merely sentenced to contribute to the building of a monastery and is permitted to marry Contarino. But her crimes are potential, rather than actual, and she can therefore be treated more leniently than Vittoria. She is certainly less eloquent than her predecessor, but that is the nature of the tragicomic genre. Hence she remains tricky and devious in her barely motivated vindictiveness, never having a chance to reach the level of introspection and self-evaluation that comes to Vittoria in her final defiance, even grandeur, in the face of death.

Echoes of *The Duchess of Malfi* are also to be found, particularly in the matters of espousal, contracting, and precontracting, as well as in the relationship of mistress and servant. To be sure, they are a conniving pair who should, as Winifrid suggests, share their guilty secrets. But there is a curious warmth born of long association between Leonora and Winifrid which at the same time offers an illuminating comment on the empty lot of the Renaissance society woman: "We have spent our life in that which least concerns life, / Only in putting on our clothes" (3.3.410–11). Despite its context it is a uniquely revealing moment of companionship comparable to those moments of tenderness between the Duchess of Malfi and Cariola at the time of her secret betrothal to Antonio (*DM* 1.1). And the resemblance does not end there. A comparison of the reactions of Leonora and Winifrid to the discovery of the false lawsuit echoes the dignity of the Duchess and the terror of Cariola at the moment of their deaths. Leonora refuses to plead for leniency; proudly she refuses to explain anything more than that Contarino is the cause of her suit against her son and says she will enter religion, while Winifrid panics, attempting to throw the blame on her mistress.

Webster's emphasis on law, on trials, and on legalism continues. The (probably) law student turned playwright continually demonstrates his familiarity with the sharp practitioners of the legal profession and skewers them lethally in his dramatic portraits, distinguishing skillfully among the law clerk with his cant terms, the "spruce" manipulations of Contilupo, and the honesty of Ariosto.[16]

Familial relationships echoing those of the earlier tragedies can also be found—inverted in the case of maternal relationship. Where Cornelia in *The White Devil* is a force for moral good, Leonora most surely is not. Brotherly tyranny in the matter of matrimonial choice is again employed, with Romelio a mercantile conglomerate of Flamineo in *The White Devil* and the Cardinal and Ferdinand in *The Duchess of Malfi*. Jolenta thus also repeats the victim-bride Vittoria and the reluctantly celibate Duchess. Even incest is not overlooked in Jolenta's claim to be with child by her brother. Similarly, Romelio's affair with the nun, Angiolella, inverts the relationship of the Cardinal and Julia in *The Duchess of Malfi*, while Jolenta's mourning ceremonial with tapers, death's head, and book recalls the Cardinal's pervertedly religious ceremonial murder of his mistress by directing her to kiss a poisoned Bible.[17]

The central action of all three independent plays concerns a dominant woman operating in defiance of established norms of feminine behavior. Each of the three heroines wishes to choose her own husband, and each flouts decorum. Vittoria is an accomplice in murder, perhaps to marry someone of higher rank, while conversely, the Duchess thinks nothing of marrying below her station to follow her heart, and Leonora opts for a much younger man, presumably for her physical gratification. But here, and this is where criticism of *The Devil's Law-Case* always founders, one cannot have any real sympathy with Leonora because she has no great moments of nobility which sear the audience. The sympathetic feminism of the two earlier plays is absent from this tragicomedy; instead, the emphasis is on the duplicity of women and those "mad tricks" by which they gain control of their husband's estates (3.1.10–30).

By the same token, the characters of the two young women in *The Devil's Law-Case* are also rather unsatisfying. Jolenta has some spirit, to be sure, and like her predecessor sister-characters she attempts to outwit and defy her brother. Yet she still allows herself to be forced into a contract with Ercole whose dogged persistence in pursuing his lady remains everlastingly surprising. She lacks the courage of those earlier women who risked much for love. Her mourning for the supposedly dead Contarino (3.3) is in Webster's best macabre style, but with extraordinary suddenness the tone shifts as Romelio and Jolenta joust—in the mode of intrigue comedy—for a position of superiority.

This same tone of incongruity is repeated at the beginning of the final act when Jolenta meets the penitent and miserable Angiolella. She acts with strange heartlessness, flippantly dismissing virginity as of little value and offering to wager on the sex of the nun's child. Similarly, her motive in misinforming Ercole, her newly-restored husband by precontract, of her own alleged pregnancy by Romelio is puzzling. Is she testing Ercole's love, does she really not wish to marry him, or is she merely being witty? Ercole's decision to marry her and her final acceptance of her faithful suitor astonish the beholder psychologically, even though the rules of dramatic symmetry are fulfilled.

The moral confusion caused by all three pairings at the end of the play is compounded by the irrelevant *sententia* of Angiolella, the last speech by a woman in the play, warning ". . . all honest virgins not to seek / The way to heaven, that is so wondrous steep, / Through those vows they are too frail to keep" (5.6.79–81). Thus the women's roles conclude with a somewhat unsatisfying moral judgment, and unsuitably mild punishments are inflicted on all the participants to satisfy the demands of tragicomedy. Yet on another level these punishments are fitting because no actual crimes have been committed. Romelio is the only exception; he who had earlier spoken against bastardy in the law-case is sentenced to make an honest woman of Angiolella, on whom he himself has fathered a bastard.[18]

To a considerable extent the difficulties of *The Devil's Law-Case* are inherent in the tragicomic genre, a hybrid which has never really caught the imagination of later audiences, or English dramatists, for that matter. The most frequent definition of tragicomedy is that of John Fletcher in his introduction to *The Faithful Shepherdess:* "A tragie-comedie is not so called in respect of mirth and killing, but in respect it wants deaths, which is inough to make it no tragedie, yet brings some neere it, which is inough to make it no comedie."[19] The beholder is supposed to remain detached, reveling in the intellectual skill with which the playwright manipulates his characters and the emotions of the audience, and finally rejoicing in the satisfying surprise of the denouement where dramatic considerations outweigh the necessities and solve the very real problems of daily life.

To be sure, there are no actual deaths in *The Devil's Law-Case,* yet the play is larded with supposed deaths, and contains three of Webster's great meditations on death and on the transitory nature of human life.

That two of these speeches belong to Romelio and one to Leonora (3.3.257–302) may seem surprising in the light of their overall character development, since Leonora plots relentlessly throughout, and Romelio begins the play as an arrogant overreacher, a sharp practitioner, one who blasphemously dares God and heaven in naming his ships, a brother who will happily sell his sister for a title since he cares little for her own desires. These flights of eloquence enforce a new evaluation of their personalities.

But these moments infiltrate the action with a strange incongruity. Romelio's first meditation on death (2.3.110–47), though a moving account of man's uncertainty about the afterlife, is nonetheless an atheistic response to the combined "deaths" of Contarino and Ercole. Similarly, his justly anthologized second peroration on the same theme comes just before his possibly fatal duel (5.4.126–43), and sounds like an honestly felt resignation to imminent confrontation with mankind's ultimate fate. But it is immediately succeeded by his herding both Leonora and the Capuchin into the closet with insulting words: "More divinity yet?" (5.4.163). Leonora's moment of mourning for the "dead" Contarino also contains elements of genuine pathos, as she contemplates her "Last merriment 'fore winter" (3.3.276), but with some shock one then realizes that not only is lust her motivation, but also that she now turns her vengeful proclivities toward her son in a reversal of her maternal affection. As with Romelio, pathos is undercut; the playwright evokes emotion and then forces instant re-evaluation of it. The momentary recognition of the human condition, demonstrated in utterances that imply the existence of an "ever-fixed mark," a navigating star, is shown to be suspect.

In effect there is no moral center to the play, a situation to some extent also found in Webster's two great tragedies. Instead there is an amoral center, an emphasis on money as evil.[20] But in the earlier tragedies this amoral centrality is partially weakened, even mitigated, by the "integrity of life" demonstrated by principal characters, particularly the Duchess of Malfi and Vittoria. Both of them depart from life with a true dignity that does much to redeem their past conduct. But in *The Devil's Law-Case,* with self-interest the major concern of the principal figures, no such accommodation is possible.

Society is evil and it remains so even though something like justice is exacted. However, it is quite clear that the central vices demonstrated— pride, greed, and lust—are endemic to a corrupt world. Traditional values such as fame, personal honor, or religion are suspect and continually called into question. But above all else, familial and human relations are shown to be wanting. No true love is demonstrated in the play, with the possible exception of Ercole, and yet he too puts his personal pride first when Jolenta expresses her preference for Contarino. The *unnatural* behavior of characters is in effect the norm, and "the Law of Nature [that] / Is the stay of the whole world . . . is broke" (4.2.264–65). Lust rules where love should live, filial and parental duties are forgotten, and fraternal affection is subordinate to acquisitiveness. Self-interest rules, except for the repentant and self-flagellating Angiolella, but even her assertion of values is speedily undercut by the flippancy of Jolenta, while her final *sententia* appears forced.

Diabolism, duplicity, disjunction, and discrepant awareness are key aspects of this curious successor to the Websterian tragedies. Instead of the inexorable progress of central figures to a fate they must confront (and in general accept with dignity) Webster presents a play based on the major device of comedic peripeteia in which actions intended to bring about evil call forth good,[21] but this device does not necessarily signify the existence of a beneficient providence. Rather, human powers, whether for evil or good, are limited in a world where relativism rules. Even the language partakes of this moral confusion "with its puns, clashing meanings, paradoxes, confusions of literal and metaphorical language, riddles."[22] And importantly, this duplicity is played out in sexual misconduct and its punning equivalent, "death." Thus lust and death both have phallic significance: Romelio's attempt to bring death by means of a poniard, for example, ironically brings about a resurrection that leads to the sexual satisfaction of his widowed mother. The desire was lethal, but the performance therapeutic. In the pattern of tragicomedy, deaths are avoided and the conclusion is huddled together largely as the result of the civil law, for once administered by an honest judge.

But even this central law-case is undercut with elements of comedy. Disguises proliferate, coincidences abound, and relevations surprise. Crispiano is resurrected, the tables are turned on Leonora, Romelio is relegitimized, and Winifrid proves to be an hilariously slippery witness as she deserts her mistress. And the entire scene is played out in front of a series of disguised persons, in whose unrecognized presence truths are revealed. Not even the end of the scene is exempt from a bifurcated view of reality as the foolish Sanitonella gloats with chauvinistic irony over this strange and unique lawsuit.

The ultimate question still remains. What exactly was Webster's purpose in this play? On that matter the critics are divided between perceiving Webster as a Christian apologist or a moral relativist.[23] The dispassionate critic (perhaps in desperation) must agree with Forker "that the text supplies warrant for both approaches," stressing the pluralistic modernity of the playwright.[24] Looked at in this manner one can begin to understand the relentless hostility (or at best puzzlement) with which this play has been either dismissed or ignored throughout the centuries.[25] Its relativism speaks to the present age, yet it is also displays kinship with the two great Websterian tragedies. But whereas Webster's "dark world is lit by a splendor that evokes something more than morbid fascination and disgust,"[26] the world of *The Devil's Law-Case* is displayed in a climate of ironic peripeteia, of tragedy subverted, of rationalism forced into a so-called happy ending.

Certainly Webster does not solve the moral and intellectual problems he raises in a truly satisfying manner. Instead, he enforces assessments upon the individual who is capable of looking at this play with rational detachment and a comedic sense of the folly (and potential wickedness) of the human condition. It still remains possible, however, for either director or audience to interpret the play as nothing more than ironic hilarity or amusing satire and hence to overlook the darker side of this extraordinarily ambivalent play.

Chapter Six
Nondramatic Works

Throughout his career John Webster was also engaged in producing introductory poems to the works of other literary collaborators and friends, prose characters, and texts for celebratory pageants and public processions. These sometimes minor works are frequently overlooked in studies of the playwright, but they do have considerable relevance to his dramatic works. At times one can see immediacy of personal observation and experience, at others borrowing from one form for another. One can also see the origins of specific dramatic characters and their attributes. Even these minor works shed some light on Webster's life, personal experience, and art.

Dedicatory Verses

The first recorded example of these works is a twelve-line commendatory poem of 1602, "To my kinde friend, Ma. An. Mundy," prefixed to the third part of *The Palmerin of England* (1602), translated by that industrious jack-of-all-literary-trades, Anthony Munday, Webster's collaborator on the lost play *Caesar's Fall* (1602). This merely efficient prefatory poem praises Munday's work for its "pith and morall discipline," and concludes with a sentiment fitting for Webster, whose knowledge of foreign and classical languages is suspect: "Translation is a traffique of high price: / It brings all learning in one Paradise."[1] Thus Webster reveals to some extent his own dependence on translations and his respect for the superior linguistic ability of others.

Webster also played some part in the publication of *Arches of Triumph,* memorializing preparations for the triumphal entry of King James I into London for his accession to the throne in 1604. A jubilant city planned a grandiose celebration. Stephen Harrison, the architect, was commissioned to design a series of seven allegorical triumphal arches through which James was to pass, pausing for poetic addresses and performances at each one. Webster's role, if any, in this official celebration is unknown, but he did contribute a graceful twenty-four line ode to preface the opulent volume, replete with excellent engravings, which recorded the proceedings and memorialized the arches of Stephen Harrison. This charming complimentary occasional poem centers on the peaceful transition of rule from the house of Tudor to that of Stuart. Other countries may celebrate bloody victories in battle but James represents the triumph of "our more civill passages of state" and demonstrates the abiding moral superiority of a thoroughly pacific England over the envy of pugnacious lands.[2]

Two other dedicatory odes must also claim attention here. The first, "To his beloved friend, Master Thomas Heywood," another of Webster's collaborators, is prefixed to that prolific author's *Apology for Actors* (1612), and is notable for an early manifestation of the respect for the acting profession that Webster showed throughout his life. Further commendatory verses to the *Apology for Actors* were contributed by Richard Perkins, who played Brachiano in *The White Devil,* and Robert Pallant, Jr., who later played Cariola in *The Duchess of Malfi.*[3] Webster comments on the text that "becomes the presse" (1.4) and supplies the actors with material that is its own praise:

> And well our Actors may approve your paines,
> For you give them authority to play,
> Even whilst the hottest plague of envy raignes;
> Nor for this warrant shall they dearly pay.
>   (11.5–8)

The second of these dedications, dated 1623 and entitled "To his industrious friend, Master Henry Cockeram," prefaced to *The English Dictionarie . . . by H. C., Gent.,* is undistinguished. These lines were omitted from all editions after the first and, to quote Lucas, "They were no great loss."[4]

A Monumental Column

On 6 November 1612, after thirteen days of agony, Henry Stuart, Prince of Wales, died of unknown causes at the age of eighteen years and nine months.[5] The young prince had been extraordinarily popular, and for good reason. Over two hundred years had passed since a new reign had promised immediate security in the person of a living and attractive male heir; no previous king to succeed *legitimately* to the throne of England had ever arrived with the succession so assured.[6]

Prince Henry had presided over a second court whose military and heroic patriotism became dangerously more attractive to many of the younger nobility than the flattery, favoritism, and stern rigor of his father's circle. Consequently, the suddenness of the young man's death prompted rumors of foul play, and a recent biographer admits that "The evidence that Henry died from natural causes is far from conclusive." King James himself was suspected of doing away with a charismatic son who was hailed as a new Hercules, the restorer of military glory, and the savior of Protestant England.[7] Prince Henry's funeral was lavish, and his coffin was adorned with a life-sized wax effigy as it was carried in procession.[8]

Webster, along with Thomas Heywood and Cyril Tourneur, joined in the national expression of grief in a collection of three elegies entitled *A Monumental Column*, issued with a date of 1613 but licensed for publication 25 December 1612.[9]

The title page reads as follows:

A / MONVMENTAL / COLUMNE, / Erected to the liuing Memory of / the euer-glorious HENRY, late / *Prince of Wales*. / Virgil. *Ostendent terris hunc tantum fata*. / *By Iohn Webster*. / *[Printer's device]* / LONDON, / Printed by N[icholas]. O[kes]. for *William Welby*, dwelling in / Pauls Church-yard at the signe of the / Swan / 1613.

Webster's contribution consists of 330 lines of rather inflated couplets. It is a "night-peece" filled with personifications, classical references, *sententiae*, similes, parables, and numerous other rhetorical devices.[10] It is also an excellent example of his use of materials borrowed from others and transmuted by the alchemy of his poetic imagination.[11] The young prince is praised as "The greatest of the Kingly Race,"[12] and in a typical Websterian juxtaposition, "a perfect Diamond set in lead" (1.4):

> . . . O all compos'd of excellent parts.
> Yong, grave *Mecœnas* of the noble Arts,
> Whose beames shall break forth from thy hollow Tombe.
> Staine the time past, and light the time to come!
> (11.275–78)[13]

Webster simultaneously perceives the essential theatricality of the prince, while emphasizing "that Henry knew the difference between court jousts and the more important spectacle of the world's great stage":[14] "Wee stood as in some spacious Theater / Musing what would become of him; his flight / Reacht such a noble pitch above our sight" (ll. 48–50).

True dedication to knightly honor, virtue, hatred of flattery, and delight in military prowess were the young man's attributes, so that he is aptly compared at length with Edward, the Black Prince, who defeated the French resoundingly at the Battle of Crécy (1396): ". . . For men thought his star / Had markt him for just and glorious war" (ll. 64–65). Webster also suggests that had their lifetimes been reversed, the Black Prince would have been evaluated in the light of Henry's achievements.[15] Yet even here his graveyard imagination can be seen when he speaks of the horrors of war with "Armes and legges, so distracted, one would say / That the dead bodies had no bodies left" (ll. 86–87).[16]

The poem also demonstrates Webster's preoccupation with the caprice of Fate and his characteristic funereal juxtapositions, particularly those of pleasure and sorrow, death and life, as shown in the reference to the postponed wedding of the Princess Elizabeth to the Elector Palatine (ll. 144–49). But then, in the traditional manner of such an elegy, the poet takes some small comfort in the fact that the dead prince has now passed beyond the clutches of slander and will live forever, his pristine virtue memorialized not in those "guilded Monuments [that] shall fall to dust" (1.321), but in the immortality of art. He has gone beyond worldly strife, and the poem ends with a sententia: *"The evening showes the day, and death crownes life."*[17] There is also an impresa, a swan, signifying the fineness of poetic style, which flies to a laurel, signifying both learning and the belief that since that tree is never struck by lightning it provides safe shelter. The poem closes with a Latin motto, *Amor est mihi causa,* "Love is my reason."

Overburian Characters

Webster had dedicated his contribution to *A Monumental Column* to Robert Carr, the notorious Viscount Rochester, and favorite of James I, perhaps looking for possible patronage. If so, Carr, the prince's rival and a sycophantic flatterer, was a curious choice, particularly in view of Webster's next work, the revision of the sixth issue of the celebrated *Characters* of Sir Thomas Overbury (1615). Overbury was a friend of Webster's in whose murder Carr and his mistress, Frances Howard,

Countess of Essex, were deeply involved. The two married, and in 1616 when an inquiry was instituted, the Countess pleaded guilty and Carr, now Earl of Somerset, was found guilty. They received a royal pardon and were imprisoned for five years in the Tower, but their agents were hanged.[18]

In early 1614 Overbury's didactic and rather dull idealized poetic portrait of *A Wife* was published and achieved instant popularity. It was reprinted almost immediately and issued with the addition of a number of prose characters. A character is basically a descriptive sketch of an individual who embodies a virtue, a vice, or a set of given qualities; the personality described is a stereotype and the purpose is basically instructive. The genre derives ultimately from the Latin writer Theophrastus, whose works popularized the form when they were translated into English in 1592, but one should not forget that Chaucer's "Prologue" to the *Canterbury Tales* is also full of "characters."

By 1615 the original twenty-one characters by Overbury and others had grown to seventy-three, including thirty-two now accepted as Webster's. He probably edited the entire text since the title page includes the motto *Non norunt haec monumenta mori* which he had affixed to his preface to *The White Devil* and was to use again in *Monuments of Honor*.[19] These additions by Webster are sometimes slighted because they compete with his three independent plays of the same period, but they are certainly worth notice because they show not only borrowings from the work of others but also parallels, sources, and influences on his dramatic works.[20] Webster offers a lively gallery of rogues, but it is his virtuous characters whose portraits have remained justly famous. In them the prose exhibits warmth, and the writer conveys a sense of real love for and understanding of his subjects. For the rogues, however, Webster generally adopts an epigrammatic, derogatory style whose bitter cleverness eventually begins to pall because of its harsh confrontational monotony.

Some of the characters are grouped opposing aspects of a given trade or profession. The first two characters are a case in point: *A worthy Commander in the Warres* and *A vaine-glorious Coward in Command.* The former is a seventeenth-century equivalent of Chaucer's ideal Knight. He cares little for ceremony, knowing that it is but a mask for the hazards of war; he shares hardships with his troops, whose welfare he does not risk unnecessarily. His commitment to a just cause is complete: "He thinkes warre is never to be given ore, but on one of these three conditions: an assured *peace,* absolute *victorie,* or an honest *death.*"[21]

The *Coward,* on the other hand, "Is one that hath bought his place, or come to it by a Noble-man's Letter" (4.26). He cares little about casualties as long as he can collect pay for his troops, but he prefers that his men die of scurvy (through malnutrition) which is less dangerous for him than battle. He supports honor and glory, but does not wish to risk his skin to attain it. "He traines by the book" (4.26), obviously paying more attention to close-order drill than preparation for battle. He is all bluster and no substance.

Three contrasting characters come from the legal profession—once again it is tempting to imagine Webster portraying persons of his own acquaintance. The first of these is *A Puny-clarke,* a lethal portrait of a half-baked farmer's son whose father wishes him to become an attorney. He is a loudmouthed glutton, a dicer, a rioter, and an inconsiderate theatergoer. This witless character fortunately never qualifies as a lawyer, unlike *A meere Petifogger,* who "Is *one of Sampsons Foxes:* He sets men together by the eares, more shamefully then *Pillories;* and in a long Vacation his sport is to goe a-Fishing *with the Penall Statutes*" (4.35). The pettifogger is a troublemaker, whether in his parish congregation or in the administration of justice, as long as he can get money. Even at the end of his life he continues in this vein by making a will so complex that no one can unravel it. Money is his lodestar and "his fingers itch after a Bribe, ever since his first practising of Court-hand" (4.35).[22] But the law is not totally composed of charlatans, as the character of *A Reverend Judge* indicates. He "Is one that desires to have his greatnesse onely measured by his goodnesse" (4.38). He is a model of upright behavior to all, and "wishes fewer Lawes, so they were better observ'd" (4.38). In judgment he errs on the side of mercy, and probity is his watchword. He speaks his mind to his prince honestly, in his virtue fearing no reprisals; "Thus honor keepes peace with him to the grave" (4.38).

Another pair of opposites are *A vertuous Widdow* and *An ordinarie Widdow.* The *vertuous Widdow* "Is the Palme-tree, that thrives not after the supplanting of her husband" (4.38). She marries only for the sake of having children, and gives herself up to works of charity in the time of her widowhood. Since the memory of her husband lies forever in her heart, she will never remarry but will live in the honor and respect of all who behold her. She is the epitome of what Saint Paul—and many writers of conduct literature—expected of women, total chastity in their widowhood. This, one will recall, is the opinion of the Duchess of Malfi's brothers when they attempt to impose their will upon her, so that this character may be read as a gloss on the same subject. Both Webster and Saint Paul also recognized the other side of the coin, however; for *An ordinarie Widdow* "The end of her husband beginnes in teares; and the end of her teares beginnes in a husband" (4.39). In other words, she marries early and often. Money is her main consideration and she is careful to keep control of her own finances while she repeatedly manipulates her way into rich matches.

Webster's gallery of rogues contains a varied collection of portraits, including *A Pirate*, "*a perpetuall plague* to noble trafique, the *Hurican of the Sea*, and the *earthquake of the Exchange*" (4.27). *An Arrant Horse-courser* is a wicked vignette rendered the more revealing when one recalls that Webster himself lived near the Smithfield horse market and must therefore have been well aware of the tricks of the trade to make an old, sluggish horse appear lively: "For powdring his eares with Quicksilver, and giving him suppositories of live Eeles he's expert" (4.31). He knows how to mask all manner of equine diseases and "onely comes short of one thing (which he despayres not utterly to bring to perfection), to make a Horse goe on a wodden legge and two crutches" (4.31).[23]

Other evildoers are *An Ingrosser of Corne*, who hoards grain in order to keep the price high, and *A Divellish Usurer*, a person universally hated. Webster here resurrects the old charge, "He puts his money to the unnatural Act of generation; and his Scrivener is the supervisor Bawd to't" (4.36). He hides his money, dresses poorly, is incapable of friendship, "And as for his death, 'tis either Surfet, the Pox, or Despaire; for seldome such as he dye of Gods making, as honest men should doe" (4.37). *A Quacksalver*, a mountebank-doctor, also meets with Webster's disapproval: "All the diseases ever sinne brought upon man, doth he pretend to bee Curer of; when the truth is, his maine cunning, is Corne-cutting" (4.40). *A Canting Rogue* is speedily dismissed, as his vagrancy and lack of honest profession warrant, while *A French Cooke* is chauvinistically treated by a true lover of English beef and mutton: "He doth not feed the belly, but the palate: and though his command lie in the Kitchin (which is but an inferiour place) yet shall you finde him a very saucy companion" (4.41).

One unexpected character in this evil company is *A Purveiour of Tobacco*, omitted from later editions of the characters, but clearly showing Webster well aware of tobacco's deleterious consequences: "He takes no long time to undoe any man hee hath to deale with, he doth it in halfe a yeare, as well as twenty; and then brags he has nipt them by the members" (4.44). Webster assigns to him an emblem of "*Dives smoaking in hell, and the word under it: Every man for himself, and the Divell for them all*" (4.44). Similar attacks on tobacco appear elsewhere in the characters of *An Ingrosser of Corne* and *A Roaring Boy,* and in two of his citizen comedy collaborations, *Westward Ho!* and *Anything for a Quiet Life,* testifying to his dislike of the weed.

Comic eccentrics are included along with rogues, notably two Dutchmen; they may suggest the influence of Webster's collaboration, Dekker, who often includes comic Hollanders in his plays. *A drunken Dutchman resident in England* notes the independence of Dutch women that Webster also remarks in *The Devil's Law-Case* (3.1.13–15) and then enlarges on the Dutch man's capacity for beer: "To conclude, the onely two plagues hee trembles at, is small Beere, and the Spanish Inquisition" (4.32). *A Button-maker of Amsterdame* is a religious hypocrite, "one that is fled over from his *Conscience,* and left his wife and children upon the Parish. / . . . and his zeale consists much in hanging his Bible in a Dutch button. . . . Lastly, his devotion is *Obstinacy,* the onely solace of his heart, *Contradiction,* and his maine end *Hypocrisie*" (4.33).

Two other juxtaposed religionists, *A Sexton* and *A Jesuite,* are treated as thoroughgoing villains. The Sexton "Is an ill-willer to humane nature" (4.41) and makes his living from the dead, either by disease or hanging. Ironically, Webster notes the seasonal nature of his profession: "Lastly, hee wishes the Dogge-daies would last all yeare long: and a great plague is his yeere of Jubile" (4.42). More bitter is Webster's assault upon the follower of Ignatius Loyola, who "Is a larger Spoone for a Traytor to feede with a Divell, than any other Order" (4.42). He meddles in business of state and uses confession as a means of controlling his flock and penance to enrich the Jesuit congregation. His dissimulation and sexual prowess are attacked, and "To conclude, would you know him beyond Sea? In his Seminary hee's a Foxe; but in the Inquisition, a Lyon Rampant" (4.42).

Of the remaining negative characters, *An Intruder into favour* is bitterly treated as one whose "passions are guided by *Pride* followed by *Injustice*" (4.29), with a final image of this flatterer as Montaigne's monkey at the top of the tree presenting his buttocks to those below. *A Roaring Boy* is a contemptuous piece, which delineates this compulsive quarreler as "a counterfeit Patent" (4.31), a cheat, a drunkard, "a *Supervisor* to Brothels" (4.31), and a bankrupt who has run through all his property. In contrast, *A Distaster of the Time* is a chronic malcontent, whose "gaule flowes as thicke in him as oile, in a poison'd stomacke. He infects all society, as Thunder sowres Wine" (4.34). The others, *A Fellow of a House, A Foote man, An Improvident young Gallant, A Water-man, An ordinary Fencer,* and *A Rimer* (or minstrel) are treated more as eccentric than wicked, though the *Water-man* has his equivalent in the modern cabdriver with his rudeness and his attempts to fleece his passengers. The *Fellow* is a poor scholar endeavoring to get ahead by his wits, a trimmer who hopes eventually to achieve a large benefice or become the chaplain to a wealthy nobleman; but all too often he enters into an unfortunate marriage. *An ordinary Fencer* merely scrapes a living by teaching the art, and comes into his own but rarely: "The Lord Maiors triumph makes him a man, for that's his best time to flourish" (4.27). The *Foote man* is the stereotypical Irish rioter, and the *Gallant* is also *A Phantastique,* a popinjay, a clotheshorse who has run through his fortune by his foolishly fashionable purchases and through his gambling at cockfights and horse races (4.32–33).

But there are also characters by Webster who are justly remembered and indeed loved. *An excellent Actor,* probably a portrait of Richard Burbage of the King's Men, presents the playwright's own ideas on acting. He insists that "By his action he [the actor] fortifies morall precepts with example; for what we see him personate, we thinke truely done before us" (4.42–43). Then as a grateful playwright he offers a generous tribute to what some people considered a profession of vagrant rogues: "Hee addes grace to the Poets labours: for what in the Poet is but ditty, in him is both ditty and musicke" (4.43). He compares the arts of painting and acting, and concludes that an excellent actor is the purest gold within the dross and as such deserves praise.[24]

A noble and retir'd Housekeeper and *A Franklin* offer another pair of affirmative portraits: they have different ranks but equally noble hearts. As Webster says of his *Franklin,* "His outside is an ancient Yeoman of England, though his inside may give armes (with the best Gentleman) and ne're fee the Herald" (4.43). The *Housekeeper,* like the *Franklin,* is *"The God of Hospitality"* (4.29), and both have such honorable souls that their word can be trusted, for pride and self-interest have no place in them. The *Franklin* also demonstrates an unexpected sense of democracy (in its modern meaning). "Though he be master he saies not to his servants goe to the field, but let us goe" (4.43); having grasped the cardinal principle of dealing justly with his inferiors, he also has no need to go to law. Cruelty is foreign to him, unless necessary for the eradication of noxious animals or the shearing of sheep; he tolerates such harmless simple pleasures as dancing in the churchyard after evensong and "thinkes not the bones of the dead any thing brused, or the worse for it" (4.44). Both men die well, and have no fear since their lives have been totally above reproach.

The most famous of all the Webster characters, *A fayre and happy Milke-mayd*, is frequently reprinted. This is a romantic and lyric evocation of a simple life lived close to the earth, totally in tune with nature and the seasons.[25] The entire character is skillfully designed, based on the passage of time, beginning with her rising at cock-crow (no slugabed she), and ending at her bedtime, making "the *Lamb* her *Courfew.*" Similarly, she is portrayed as living through a week of innocent dreams to Friday's dream "that shee conceales for fear of anger" (4.30). Finally "She may dye in the *Spring-time,* to have a store of flowers stuck upon her winding-sheete" (4.30). Thus the character of the *Milke-mayd* also becomes a paradigm of the life of an innocent soul whose virtues are those of a true Christian: humility, innocence, diligence, chastity, modesty, sympathy, and dedication to duty within her assigned station in life. She is totally in harmony with herself and the divine plan for nature.

This section on the characters thus ends fittingly with Webster's supreme effort in the genre. However, one should also examine the grotesques to appreciate Webster's effective use of the epigram, his unexpected turns of phrase, the rhetorical flourishes, and the puns. He skewers pretension with wit, and when that becomes repetitive, he often saves the day with a shrewd observation that goes beyond the commonplace book and evokes some of the teeming life of his own London. His prose can be economical and lively; on other occasions he demonstrates surprising and often hilarious juxtapositions that emphasize the disjunctive nature of his dramatic art. The character may be a minor genre, but it certainly was conducive to the writing of good modern prose, and Webster is by no means an unworthy contributor to it.

Monuments of Honor

After his part in the celebrations surrounding the coronation of James I and his contribution to *A Monumental Column* (1612), Webster may have hoped for employment on public celebrations, most notably the Lord Mayor's Procession. Certainly his connection with the Merchant Taylors' ought to have proved useful when a member of that guild was elected Lord Mayor, but he was unsuccessful on three such occasions: in 1602 and 1605, for Sir Robert Lee and Sir Leonard Halliday, respectively, when his collaborator Anthony Munday was granted the honor; and again in 1612, when another collaborator, Thomas Dekker, wrote the pageant for Sir John Swinnerton.[26] Not until 1624, with the installation of Sir John Gore, was Webster successful with his *Monuments of Honor.* In 1630, Sir Henry Ducy, another member of the Merchant Taylors', was elected Lord Mayor, but Webster was again passed over— if he had not already died.

Monuments of Honor was a highly ambitious and expensive undertaking, its magnificence justified by the fact that though the Merchant Taylors' were a powerful guild, they had not had a Lord Mayor elected from their ranks for a dozen years. Consequently the Merchant Taylors' poured out over £1,000 for the celebration, their largest sum in three hundred years.[27] The magnificence of the show can be gleaned from the title page of the published version.

[Monuments of Honor]. / Deriued from remarkable Antiquity, and / Celebrated in the Honorable City of *London,* at the / sole Munificent charge and expences of the / Right Worthy and Worshipfull Fraternity, of / the Eminent Merchant-taylors. / Directed in their most affectionate Loue, at the / *Confirmation of their right Worthy Brother* / Iohn Gore in the High Office of His / *Maiesties Li[eu]tenant ouer this His Roy[a]ll / Chamber.* / Expressing in a Magnificent Tryumph, all the Pageants, / *Chariots of Glory, Temples of Honor, besides a* / specious and goodly Sea Tryumph, as well particularly / to the Honor of the City / as generally to the Glory of this our Kingdome. / *Invented and Written by* Iohn Webster / Merchant-Taylor / ————*Non norunt haec monumenta mori* / [Device: Arms of the Merchant Taylors' Company] / *Printed at* London *by* Nicholas Okes, 1624.

The show began early on 29 October 1624 when the new mayor and his retinue took to the water in a series of barges for their progress up the river to Westminster where he took his oath of office at the Exchequer. Then on their return they disembarked at St. Paul's Wharf and rode in procession through Cheapside.[28] Celebrations continued into the evening. For the upriver passage Webster "fashioned . . . upon the water two Eminent Spectacles, in maner of a Sea-Triumph."[29] The first of these two barges contained four persons, *Oceanus* and *Thetis,* the sea nymph, in the front, with the Rivers Thames *(Themesis)* and Medway, over which the Lord Mayor had jurisdiction, behind. The second barge held "a faire Terrestriall Globe, Circled about, in convenient Seates, with seaven of our most famous [English] navigators" (ll. 27–29). Introduced by "a peale of sea-Thunder from the other side the water" (1. 38), Thetis, in a charming conceit, suggests that this is Venice during the celebrated annual ceremonial of that city's marriage to the sea. Oceanus, however, enlightens her: *"That beautious seate is London"* (1. 50). He introduces the other figures on all the barges, detailing the power of the Lord Mayor, the achievements of the navigators, and above all else, emphasizing their honor. Thetis having given her blessing, the barges were then taken ashore "and in convenient place employed for adorning the rest of the Triumph" (11. 86–87). This amphibious show must have been a remarkable feat.

The next spectacle took place in St. Paul's churchyard, a *"Temple of Honor,* the Pillars of which are bound about with Roses, and other beautifull Flowers, which shoot up to the adorning of the Kings Maiesties Armes on the top of the Temple" (11. 90–94). Here Webster presented Troynovant, New Troy or London, perpetuating the strained legend that the city was founded by descendants of Brut after the fall of Troy. Beneath her sat Antwerp, Paris, Rome, Venice, and Constantinople in adoring fashion. "Under these sit five famous Schollers and Poets of this our Kingdome" (11. 98–99), constituting an interesting piece of literary criticism: Geoffrey Chaucer, John Gower, John Lydgate, Sir Thomas More, and Sir Philip Sidney. Riding before this Temple came a procession of founders and important past members of the Merchant Taylors' introduced by Sir John Hawkwood, the famous leader of the White Company in Italy, who, according to legend, had been apprenticed to a tailor.[30]

After him came "a Triumphant *Chariot* with the Armes of the Merchant-Taylors" (11. 160–61) containing the eight kings of England who were members "free" of the company. Each of them is given a sometimes surprising thumbnail sketch.

First the Victorious *Edward* the Third, that first quartered the Armes of *France* with those of *England,* next the munificent *Richard* the Second, ... the Grave and Discreet *Henry* the *Fourth,* . . . the Scourge and Terrour of *France, Henry* the Fifth . . . his religious, though unfortunate Sonne, *Henry* the sixt: . . . the Amarous and Personable *Edward* the Fourth . . . the bad man, but the good King, *Richard* the Third; . . . the wise and politique *Henry* the seaventh, houlding the Charter by which the Company was Improved. . . . (11. 169–82)

Distinctions are made between the Lancastrian (red roses) and Yorkist (white roses) monarchs, with Henry VII praised for uniting both factions.

Webster relates this to the motto James I had devised for the gold coin of his own reign: *"Henricus rosas regna Jacobus,"* Henry united the Roses, James the kingdoms [of England and Scotland] (1. 189). Edward III speaks this part of the pageant with all the kings repeating the English translation of the Merchant Taylors' motto: "By unity the smallest things grow great" (1. 203), *Concordia parvae res crescunt* (1. 205).

Behind this conclave of kings came Anne, wife of Richard II, together with noblewomen who were free of the Company (11. 206–7).[31] They were followed by assorted nobles and churchmen to make up a total of around one hundred in this section alone. Then, to celebrate the Merchant Taylors' ancient connection with the Fraternity of St. John the Baptist and the Knights of St. John of Jerusalem, two famous representatives of those orders were included, Jean Parisot de la Valette, defender of Malta against the Turks in 1565, and Amadeus V of Savoy, the popularly accepted defender of Rhodes against the same enemy in 1315. This procession was followed in turn by "the Shippe called the *Holy-Lambe"* (11. 235–36), large enough to be floated but small enough to be kept suspended in the rafters of the Company's hall until brought out on such ceremonial occasions to fire a celebratory broadside.[32] Finally, this part of the pageant ended with a lion and a camel to signify the inclusiveness of the Merchant Taylors' interests.

The fourth pageant was "the *Monument of Charity* and *Learning*—this fashioned like a beautiful Garden with all kind of flowers" (11. 243–44), with singing birds so as to give the illusion of spring in winter. There, seated under an elm tree, sat Sir Thomas White, Merchant Taylor, supporter of Gloucester Hall, Oxford, and legendary founder of Saint John's College (though this is disputed).

The final and climactic pageant, entitled *Monument of Gratitude,* presented the late Prince Henry enthroned on a rock of jewels, who though dead since 1612 (the year of the last Merchant Taylors' mayor), was still remembered by Webster as the epitome of all kingly virtues. Under a canopy of half a celestial globe, in the midst of which hung an image of the Holy Lamb in sunbeams, sat the Prince, dressed in his Garter robes, while grouped below him were personifications of the important monarchical qualities: Magistracy, Liberality, Navigation, Unanimity, Industry, Chastity, Justice, Obedience, Peace, and Fortitude, all with iconographical and heraldic attributes. The speech for this pageant was delivered by "Amade le Graunde," Amadeus V of Savoy, to celebrate the gratitude of England that such a paragon of princely virtue was briefly permitted to illumine the land with his priceless and perfect brand of potential monarchical perfection.[33]

The dead Prince Henry thus becomes the focal point of the entire pageant, and the central theme is his embodiment of all the virtues earlier portrayed. The celebration culminates in this resplendent and glittering float of Gratitude, which was illuminated at night. In it Webster skillfully manages, with the greatest diplomacy, to draw very specific political comparisons with the corruption of James's court where the current heir apparent (the future Charles I) and his father were at loggerheads. In this London spectacle Webster returned inconsolably to the theme of his earlier work, *A Monumental Column,* in an extraordinarily lavish and masterly use of mixed media for the purpose of political propaganda, while celebrating the Merchant Taylors' of which he was proud to say he was "borne free." One wonders why after such a manifest, though expensive, success Webster did not write the pageant for the installation of Sir Henry Ducy in 1630. Perhaps he was ill, or already dead.

Verses on an Engraving of King James I and His Family, Living and Dead

A final piece of funerary poetry completes Webster's career in the nondramatic, public mode. It consists of verses on an engraving picturing the entire family of James I, with the dead identified by skulls. No copy of the original engraving, made a month before the end of James's reign, is extant, but the version of 1633 (used here as frontispiece) bears under the verses this notation: "Haec composuit Ioannes Webster."[34] The sentiments expressed are eminently conventional and derivative in their animadversions on malign Fate and capricious Fortune, while the verses themselves are quite forgettable. Nonetheless, their juxtaposition with this curiously macabre portrait has a certain Websterian appropriateness.

Chapter Seven
Final Period: Collaborations and Conjectural Works

After the fine creative fury of his three independent plays Webster returned to his early practice of collaboration in his final period. He had worked before with Dekker and Middleton, and Thomas Heywood was an old friend. New to him are William Rowley, John Ford, and Philip Massinger. Once again Webster responds to popular taste; his unique dark vision has been submerged in chameleonlike collaboration. Only in *Appius and Virginia* is there an echo of the earlier high seriousness and a courtroom scene capable of comparison with *The White Devil* or *The Devil's Law-Case*.

Nonetheless, these doubtful plays repay study. In this chapter, those works generally accepted as substantially by Webster are given detailed analysis, in their supposed order of composition, together with comments on their authorship even if there is no corroborative external evidence for Webster's participation in them. Some works formerly assigned to Webster and now considered spurious are discussed in the final section.

Anything for a Quiet Life

Text, date, source, and authorship. This play was not published until 1662, with authorship assigned to Thomas Middleton who had died in 1627. The title page reads:

ANY THING / FOR A / QUIET LIFE. / A / COMEDY, / Formerly Acted at *Black-Fryers*, by His / late Majesties Servants, / *Never before Printed*. Written by *Tho. Middleton*, Gent. / [Printer's Device]. *London:* Printed by *Tho. Johnson* for *Francis Kirkman*, and *Henry Marsh*, and / are to be sold at the *Princes Arms* in / *Chancery-Lane*. 1662.

Kirkman is untrustworthy, and since the provenance and vicissitudes of the manuscript are unknown, one cannot tell how much of the text is original or how badly it has been corrupted by playhouse, scribal, and printing house alterations. The only available details of the first performance are those of the title page, where the actual date does not appear, but on the basis of internal evidence it is usually assigned to 1621–22. The plot is of unknown origin and is probably an invention of the authors, who, as Lucas comments, "had no great cause to be proud of it."[1]

There is no external evidence to link Webster with this play, so its attribution to Middleton even by the untrustworthy Francis Kirkman remained unquestioned until 1921, when H. Dugdale Sykes suggested Webster's hand. Certainly, there are parallels with the Overburian characters and *The Duchess of Malfi,* together with borrowings from such other favorite Webster sources as the *Arcadia* of Sir Philip Sidney.[2] However, some echoes of *The Duchess* may have originated with Middleton, who is known to have admired it, and who wrote one of the introductory poems to the published text of 1623. Overall, the exact contribution of Webster to this play is difficult to assess, but recent linguistic analyses, combined with internal evidence drawn from borrowings and parallels, indicate that something in the nature of forty-five percent of the total play is probably by him.[3]

Synopsis.   The four levels of plotting in this play are skillfully juggled by means of alternating scenes. The first concerns the folly of the recently widowed Sir Francis Cressingham, an elderly alchemist and gamester, in marrying a fifteen-year-old girl. She immediately sends the two younger children of Cressingham to board with Water Chamlet, a rich mercer. To indulge her expensive tastes she convinces her husband to allow the destruction of his alchemical equipment, and then strips him of all his lands and goods, suggesting that he should live a retired life on a small pension.

The second plot is that of Mr. Water Chamlet, the mercer, married to a shrewish woman named Rachel. He generously takes in the children of Cressingham when they are turned away by their stepmother, but his wife charges that they are his own bastards. With that, she flounces off to the house of her brother, Knavesbee, threatening to gain a divorce, leaving the cloth dealer totally devastated; he can be happy neither with nor without her.

In yet a third plot, the aptly named Knavesbee attempts to prostitute his wife to Lord Beaufort. At first appalled, she then agrees, despite her husband's "base contemptible nature," hoping to gain rich jewels and fine clothes from her "lover." As she waits for the nobleman, she sees his page, Selenger, and insists that he is the person she wants to bed, refusing Lord Beaufort and asking him to procure the servant for her. When she returns to her husband, he quite joyfully accepts his self-chosen lot as pander, cuckold, and wittol, but she now refuses to sleep with him because of his social inferiority. She says she has lain with a lord.

The fourth plot concerns Young Franklin, an impecunious sea captain looking for money. He decides to gull some wealthy fool and chooses Water Chamlet as his candidate. Scenes of fast talking, sharp practice, low apprentice comedy, and fractured French ensue, involving Young Franklin, and his companion, Young George Cressingham. The second plot now impinges on the fourth with the return of the shrewish Rachel Chamlet to save her husband from marrying a French bawd.

Act 5 unravels all the remaining complications. Old Franklin arrives, in mourning for his "dead" son, accompanied by Young Cressingham and an old serving man (that same son in disguise). When he offers to pay off his son's creditors at fifty percent of indebtedness, they jump at the chance, reasoning that since the young man is "dead" they are lucky to get anything. The other aspects of the multiple plot are now equally confused. Young Cressingham upbraids his cruel mother-in-law for her mistreatment of his father and his siblings; George, an apprentice, has been turned away by Mistress Chamlet for his part in attempting a reconciliation; and Beaufort attacks Knavesbee for having a strumpet for a wife, because she has gone to bed with the page.

Suddenly Mistress Knavesbee appears, along with the page, who is revealed to be a girl in disguise. Rachel Chamlet agrees to take George back into service. Old Cressingham is discovered well dressed and still in possession of his estates, which have been bought and cared for by Franklin. Then Lady Cressingham appears with the two young children, well dressed and "very gallant." Her actions were designed to force her husband to abandon his addictions to alchemy and gaming. Then, but only after gaining a full public release from all his son's creditors, Franklin reveals that his scapegrace son lives. The play ends with the wish that everyone will henceforth lead quiet lives.

Critical Comments. This play is usually dismissed as an unworthy effort, largely because of the complex and unmotivated conclusion. But mystification of the audience is the chief device of the piece, with the character of Lady Cressingham a good example. Her lovestruck husband continually praises her gravity and good judgment, but because he is behaving in such an eminently foolish fashion, no one believes him, while the evidence of her behavior also runs counter to such praise.

Scenes are played without explanation or hint, in particular the scene with Selenger, the girl disguised as a page, who is appalled at Mistress Knavesbee's apparent lust, excoriating her in lines reminiscent of *The White Devil:* "filthy/Beauty, what a white witch thou art!" (3.1.88–89). Here, insofar as the audience knows, Sib has indeed fallen for the nubile "boy," a situation that makes her no less reprehensible than her "contemptible" husband.

Once again, as is common in the work of Webster, we have strong women characters who form the mainspring of the entire plot. The men may say more, but the basic machinery of events is put in motion by the women and the men merely react. The influence of the Overburian characters is also notable, for Lady Cressingham is portrayed until act 5 as the opposite of Overbury's idealistic poetic fiction, "A Wife." Similarly, Young Cressingham's attack on her is constructed in the manner of a Character of a Cruel Mother-in-Law (5.1.241–70), while Mistress Rachel Chamlet epitomizes the shrew. Yet curiously, all these women appear to love their worthless or foolish husbands, and like the general run of wives in citizen comedy, all remain chaste.

The central topics of the play are those of Middleton and citizen comedy in general—sex and money. Greed is the besetting sin of all the fools of the play; those who put their faith entirely in money are gulled. But as with other plays in the manner of Middleton there is no real moral center to the play because of the playwrights' detachment and many-faceted vision. Characters are treated equally in a nonjudgmental manner; individual points of view cancel each other out. Old Franklin, for instance, who appears only in the last act of the play, is praised for his role in maintaining the property of Sir Francis Cressingham, yet he engages in some very sharp practices by paying off his son's creditors under false pretenses, forcing them to agree to halve their demands. Presumably this is their punishment for greed. Similarly, Water Chamlet is cozened as a result of his own desire for wealth. In his role as the hopelessly henpecked husband he ought to be a figure of ridicule, with his frequent quotation of the play's title, *Anything for a Quiet Life,* yet his folly is balanced by eminently charitable behavior toward the children of Cressingham. Another morally ambivalent character is Lord Beaufort, who begins the play as the epitome of good sense when remonstrating with Sir Francis Cressingham, but who is later revealed as an old lecher.

Thus the audience is frequently unable to decide which of its mixed responses to accept. The puzzlement is compounded by the "detective story" approach to the plotting. Hints are dropped, and then left undeveloped until that aspect of the action is completed; false leads are given, motivation is murky, and evidence is withheld. Nonetheless, there are very many amusing moments, even if bawdy puns and double meanings are sometimes carried to extremes—another characteristic failing of both Webster and Middleton. The Chamlet cozening scene (2.2), the skeinwinding scene with the Page and Mistress Knavesbee (3.1), and the scene of the barber and Ralph at cross purposes (2.3), still cause mirth. These scenes derive from jestbook tales, and though contributing something to the development of the four-level plot, they can almost stand alone as vaudeville skits. In short, the one thing this many-faceted play does not provide the theatergoer is what it promises in the title, *Anything for a Quiet Life.*

A Late Murther of the Son Upon the Mother, or Keep the Widow Waking

A considerable amount of evidence has been pieced together concerning this lost play. Commissioned by Ralph Savage of the Red Bull playhouse, it was a collaborative venture by Thomas Dekker, John Ford, William Rowley, and John Webster, to exploit two very recent and notorious crimes. The first was a murder of 9 April 1624, in which a Whitechapel youth named Nathaniel Tindall stabbed his mother to death. No motive is known, but he pleaded guilty at his trial at the Old Bailey and was hanged in his own neighborhood as an evil example.

The second of these crimes involved a case of matrimonial entrapment that has gained in interest since the discovery that Webster may well have been acquainted with the participants, who resided in his parish of St. Sepulchre's. In July 1624 Anne Elsdon, a wealthy widow of sixty-two, fell in love with Tobias Audley, a seller of tobacco and drink, a young man in his twenties with an evil reputation. Audley brought the widow to a tavern in Blackfriars and there, in the company of four of his friends, managed to keep her drunk for five days. During this time he refused to allow her to return home, tricked her into a witnessed contract of marriage, bought a license with her own money and found a priest to marry them before she was sober enough to make an informed decision. By the time the widow realized what had happened, the marriage had been consummated, Audley had stripped her house of its valuables, and she was the laughing stock of the conspirators who were now ill treating her.

By now Benjamin Garfield, the husband of Mrs. Elsdon's only child, Elizabeth, had discovered her plight, and initiated the first of a series of lawsuits to recover the pillaged property. Dissatisfied with the law's delay, he eventually brought the case to the Court of Star Chamber, but unfortunately both Elsdon and Audley died before a decision was reached. Audley was in Newgate prison at the time of his death, but was never convicted, while poor Mistress Elsdon was living in what was left of her ransacked house. The misappropriated property was not recovered, but lawsuits continued as Garfield objected to the libellous treatment of his mother-in-law on the stage. He sued the playwrights Rowley and Dekker, the business manager of the Red Bull, Ralph Savage, the playhouse builder, Aaron Holland, and Ellis Worth, an actor of the company. It is from Dekker's evidence in this lawsuit that something of this lost potboiler can be reconstructed.[4]

Dekker and Rowley were apparently responsible for the overall plotting, combining the two crimes and using the Elsdon case as comic relief. Thus the emphasis was on the folly of the widow and the enterprise of the exploitive young man. This was how the poor woman was treated in a broadside ballad on the subject. On the other hand, two ballads on the Tindall murder are tearjerkers emphasizing the repentance of the criminal. The dramatized contrast must have made for striking theatrical effect. Apparently Dekker wrote the first act to introduce the two plots, and then each collaborator contributed a single act, with all working together on the final one. Speed was essential, for the events of the Elsdon case began in late July 1624 and the play was licensed for performance between 3 and 15 September when the principals were both still alive. Clearly this opportunistic combination of murder, sex, repentance, chicanery, and intense local topicality was a natural for the popular audience of the Red Bull.

A Cure for a Cuckold

Text, date, sources, and authorship. Like its predecessor, *Anything for a Quiet Life,* this play was published in 1661 by Francis Kirkman. He attributed it to Webster and Rowley and prefaced the publication with a piece of advertising puffery, claiming that *"several persons remember the Acting of it, and say that it then pleased generally well"* and adding the astonishing assertion that *"The Expedient of Curing a Cuckold (after the maner set down in this* Play) *hath bin tried to my knowledge, and therefore I may say* Probatum est."[5]

The title page reads as follows:

A / CURE / FOR A / CUCKOLD. / A PLEASANT / COMEDY, / As it hath been several times Acted / with great Applause. / *Written by* John VVebster *and* / VVilliam Rowley. / *Placere Cupio.* / London, Printed by *Tho. Johnson,* and are to be sold by *Francis / Kirkman,* at his Shop at the sign of *John Fletchers Head,* / over against the Angel-Inne, on the Back-side of / St. *Clements,* without *Temple-Bar,* 1661.

Since the immediate source of the play was probably *The Parliament of Love* (1624) by Philip Massinger, *A Cure for a Cuckold* probably dates from late 1624 to early 1625; it can hardly be later than 1626, the date of Rowley's death.[6] Massinger employs a theme similar to one already used by John Marston in *The Dutch Curtezan* (1603), but this too had been borrowed, from "The Disordred Life of the Countess of Celant," translated into English almost simultaneously by William Painter in the *Palace of Pleasure* (1566–67, 2:24), and Geoffrey Fenton in *Certain Tragicall Discourses* (1567). In turn their source was the *Histoires Traqiques* of Francois de Belleforest (1565, 2:20), the moralizing adapter of *novelle* by the Italian writer Matteo Bandello (in this case *Novella* 2:4).[7]

The tale of this insatiate countess concerns Bianca Maria Scappardona, the daughter of a rich usurer, initially married to a viscount who allowed her little freedom, fearing her sensual appetite. After his death she married the Count of Celant, leaving him for a series of lovers in Padua. For a year she was with Ardizzino Valperga, but then became attracted to his friend, Roberto Sanseverino. Angered, Valperga left her and publicized her immorality. In revenge, Bianca Maria asked Sanseverino to kill his friend, but he hesitated, weighing the prior claims of amity. As a result, Bianca Maria returned to Valperga, and pressured him to kill Sanseverino, but when the two friends discovered her duplicity they both proceeded to inform the world. She then found a third lover, Don Pietro di Cardona, in Milan, and persuaded him to kill Valperga. After Don Pietro was arrested, he confessed and escaped punishment, but the countess was beheaded outside the Citadel.

Webster had already gone to the same sources for *The Duchess of Malfi,* but this time he has taken only some of the action, the two duels, and the conflict of lust/love and friendship, translating them not only into England, but also into the Fletcherian mode of tragicomedy. This may be the result of his collaboration with Rowley, or a concession to popular taste, because the locale does not dictate genre. Kirkman's assignment of authorship to Webster and Rowley is now generally accepted, despite some skepticism in the past, although some slight contribution from the hand of Thomas Heywood has also been proposed.[8] As a rough division of authorial labor, it is fair to say that Webster was responsible for the main plot of the play and Rowley for the subplot of the merrily bawdy and humane character of the mariner, Compass, a role he probably wrote for himself as a specialist in fat clown roles.

Synopsis. This play divides neatly into two plots, differentiated by social class. At the marriage of Annabel Woodroff and Bonvile, Lessingham declares his love to Clare who says she will never marry. She gives him a speedy reply to his suit in the form of a riddling letter: *"Prove all thy friends, finde out the best and nearest, / Kill for my sake that Friend that loves thee dearest"* (1.1.118–19). Lessingham tests all of his friends, telling them that he must fight a duel and requires a second who, contrary to the usual rules of dueling, must also fight. He is refused by all except Bonvile, who defers the consummation of his marriage to the claims of friendship. He then sends Annabel a letter willing all his possessions to her. When Clare discovers this, she claims that Lessingham has misunderstood her letter and fears that both young men are lost. Arrived at the dueling site, Lessingham tells Bonvile that they are to be the duelists. Although admiring his friend's self-sacrificial virtue, he allows the superiority of the claims of love. He will kill Bonvile and fulfill Clare's instructions.

Bonvile, naturally eager to save his life, shrewdly interprets the letter and suggests that Clare wishes Lessingham to kill the "self-love, or pride" (3.1.87) within his heart. Then, he emphasizes the choice between love and friendship by offering him his sword. Lessingham cannot commit cold-blooded murder, and with supersubtle skill, Bonvile once again resorts to legal hairsplitting to prove that since Lessingham has slain their friendship, they must henceforth be enemies.

Meanwhile, the deserted but patiently unquestioning Annabel goes in search of her errant bridegroom, only to be set upon by Rochfield, a younger brother who, having no prospects of advancement, has reluctantly decided to become a thief.[9] Then when a sailor appears bearing a license to privateer, Rochfield, along with the other gallants, Woodroff, and Annabel herself, invests in the enterprise. The privateer unexpectedly falls in with three Spanish men of war, and Rochfield is instrumental in taking the Spaniards in prize. His noble blood triumphs, he makes his own fortune, forswears knavery and turns a very handsome profit for all the investors.

The subplot is tied to the main plot by the very tenuous device of Master Franckford, brother to Annabel's father, and his barren wife, Luce. She, knowing her infirmity, allows her husband, "within compass," to seek his procreative pleasure elsewhere. This he has done in the person of Urse, also known as Mistress Compass, wife to a seaman who has been absent for four years and is believed drowned. Franckford has had a son by her, whom he proudly supports. However, Master Compass suddenly reappears, and with extraordinary understanding and tolerance, wishes to take back his wife, forgiving her fault and quite happily accepting the child as his own.

Compass and his wife try to gain custody and confront the Franckfords, each claiming to "own" the infant, Franckford by right of begetting, and Compass because of the labor of his wife in bringing it into the world. The situation calls for a Solomon, so both go to law. Franckford claims paternity on the grounds that he has settled money on the child, and his wife argues their higher social status. Compass, Woodroff and Counsel agree that custody should be awarded to the father, who is obliged to support his child, even an illegitimate one, suggesting as precedent that the crops of the earth belong to the farmer, not the earth that brought them forth. This angers Compass, who reduces the whole argument to absurdity by asking who keeps the piglets if a stray boar impregnates his sow. This display of hilarious common sense disarms everyone. The lawyers reverse themselves, Compass is permitted to keep the child, and Frankford generously agrees to pay the promised settlement.

Raymond, one of the newly rich gallants, now suggests a parodic legal maneuver to "cure" Compass's cuckoldry. The seaman and his wife should divorce and immediately remarry as persons in a different state of life. Once again the action turns on verbal manipulation, because Compass will get dead drunk and awaken a new man, and Urse will drown herself in tears as a new-made widow. At the end of two hours they will meet, woo each other, and then remarry. Cuckoldry is "cured" in the legal sense by understanding, toleration, and most important of all, a good sense of the hilarity and inevitability of human frailty.

Interspersed with the Compass plot are the continuing confusions of the upper classes. The fickle Clare cannot be pleased, and hints that she may marry Lessingham. More verbal hairsplitting ensues when Bonvile the Bridegroom tries to convince Clare to renounce her foolish passion for him and marry his friend. But now both men spurn Clare. In a further proliferation of confusions Lessingham seeks revenge on Bonvile for alienating Clare's affections, while Bonvile suspects Annabel of infidelity with Rochfield. Finally, all are reconciled after Rochfield tells of Annabel's part in rescuing him from a life of crime. Clare then repents, while Lessingham willingly accepts her as his wife.

But the last word belongs to the merrily tolerant Compass as he proceeds to the church once again: "And so, good night, my Bride and Ile to bed: / He that has Horns, thus let him learn to shed" (5.1.521–22).

Critical comments. This tragicomedy offers a singularly complicated and preposterous plot based on the conflict of love and friendship together with a subplot filled with skillful legal satire based on the twisting of text and precedent. These scenes probably made use of Webster's legal expertise, whether or not he actually wrote all of them. The main plot also employs quasilegal techniques of setting "the word against the word," developing subtle interpretations to suit the individual's purpose,[10] and even using the hoary old device of the riddling, or mispunctuated letter (1.1.118–19).

To some extent *A Cure for a Cuckold* may seem out of character for Webster, but it follows with a certain logic from the legal maneuvering of *The Devil's Law-Case,* while the mixed tone of the play, alternating between tragicomic main plot and almost burlesque subplot, is analogous to his disjunctive tragic approach. As in the earlier work, Webster plays on multiplicities of response by means of ironic juxtapositions. The would-be thief, Rochfield, speaks movingly about the plight of a younger brother (2.1.1–22) and the terrors of criminal life (2.4.101–20) while he contemplates violence, but in moments of danger his noble blood triumphs. The jilted Lessingham becomes a hostile malcontent and dilates on the value of friendship at the moment of the duel (3.1.35–65), only to be saved by his friend's interpretation of Clare's riddle. Equivocation, usually something to be despised, is turned to good purposes in this play.

Once again there are some important women characters: Clare who is so capriciously manipulative that she turns the main plot into almost irreconcilable turmoil; Annabel who develops resourcefulness and exhibits extraordinary patience as the complications multiply; and two others from the subplot: the tolerantly long-suffering, barren Luce, and Urse, the wife of Compass, morally frail, but gifted with self-knowledge and a strong sense of the comedy of human existence. However, amusing though the outcome is, the play presents critical problems because of the contrasting, even clashing approaches endemic to tragicomedy.[11]

To some extent the structural difficulty of *A Cure for a Cuckold* is compounded by the probable division of compositional labor between Webster and Rowley. As a result, the almost self-sufficient, earthy bawdry of Rowley's Compass subplot has sometimes been denigrated, even to the extent of splitting it off from the main plot.[12] But this however is a misguided exercise in snobbery and prudery, because the lower-class Compass scenes ring changes on the verbal devices of the main plot and offer a real contribution to the fun of the play that arises from its total divorce from, and parodic inversion of, everyday logic.

Both parts of the play study the theme of human relationships and both employ exaggeration as a dominant device. The main plot concerns itself with the process of finding one's true emotional center whether in love or in friendship. Too much self-absorption brings about near disaster, and the long-suffering goodness of Annabel is the only constant to be found in this portion of the action. The subplot, on the other hand, turns this view upside down. Compass is a merry and hyperbolically long-suffering soul, with a solution recognizing the comic fact of human existence that error is its only constant and nothing human is alien. That this is a central point is clearly signaled by the number of times the word "compass" is used in the sense of a guide or limit in both portions of the text.

Far from writing perfunctorily in this play, Webster makes sophisticated use of tragicomedy to criticize the genre itself, and at the same time to question accepted ideals. His parodic verbal manipulation and prevarication pervade the play, with inversion and the provision of improbable solutions leading the thoughtful members of the audience to examine ideals and then reassess them. Once again, Webster has led his beholders into a wilderness where traditional values do not run and where tolerance raised to a comic degree is the solution to the labyrinthine complications of the plot. If that is the Compass that guides to the "safe" haven of matrimony, the usual conclusion to comedy is here left open to doubt. The jokes on the inevitability of cuckoldry emphasize that fact.

A Cure for a Cuckold represents the comic obverse of Webster's dark view of the universe; in this underrated play he reaches his peak as a collaborative writer of tragicomedy. One may complain that he and Rowley *ought* to have offered a conventionally moral solution, but in the words of Oscar Wilde, "The truth is rarely pure, and never simple." *A Cure for a Cuckold* denies easy accommodation but nonetheless hints at the most difficult one of all, acceptance of humanity as something less than ideal.

The Fair Maid of the Inn

Text, date, sources, and authorship. This play was licensed for performance by the King's Men at the Blackfriars theater on 22 January 1625–26. The sole author was then listed as John Fletcher, ironically the one person now considered to have a very minor role in the writing, perhaps contributing only a portion of 4.1. When first published in 1647, in the first folio edition of the works of Francis Beaumont and John Fletcher, *The Fair Maid of the Inn* was again assigned to Fletcher. Critics now divide the play among Philip Massinger, John Ford, John Fletcher, and perhaps John Webster.

Although Webster is usually credited with creating Forobosco (a name appearing in *DM* 2.2.31) and the scenes in which he appears, the exact nature of his contribution remains so uncertain that some authorities prefer not to admit the play into the canon. Indeed, no external evidence connects him either with the play, or with the King's Men at that time, although he had earlier collaborated on *The Malcontent* for them. Further, some of the echoes of Websterian plots, themes, or verbal tricks could be the result of the playwright's influence on other writers. Nonetheless there is a persistent tradition, originally based on evidence drawn from verbal parallels but more recently bolstered by careful linguistic analysis of Webster and his collaborators, which allows *The Fair Maid of the Inn* at least a qualified acceptance as partly Webster's work.[13]

Certainly, Webster had already used some of the sources and devices employed in this play, in particular Mariana's disowning of her son, Cesario, which recalls *The Devil's Law-Case*. *The Duchess of Malfi* is echoed in the hints of incest between Cesario and his sister, Clarissa. The tale of the lovers Biancha and Cesario is new, based very loosely on *La Illustre Fregona,* one of the *Novelares Exemplares* of Miguel de Cervantes, in which two young men go off on a spree. The hero, after falling in love with a maidservant in an inn, takes service there and persuades his friend to join him. Finally they are discovered by their fathers and when the girl is found to be the long-lost sister of the friend, marriage ensues.

Synopsis. Cesario, son to Alberto, Admiral of Venice, has assumed the office of guardian of his sister's chastity. Clarissa, however, censures him for his love affair with Biancha, the Fair Maid of the Inn, because of her low birth. Cesario praises the young lady's beauty and virtue and then forces Clarissa to swear never to love without his consent. As a token of this bargain he gives her a ring, kissing her hand with a comment hinting at more than brotherly affection: "Which were it not my sisters, I should kisse / With too much heate" (1.1.135–36).

In the next scene Alberto and his friend Baptista extol the virtues of war. Then Baptista recounts the tale of his secret second marriage, disastrously terminated by the Duke of Milan, the bride's father. Within Alberto's family, Mariana, his wife, reveals herself as an overprotective mother, excessively and perhaps pervertedly devoted to her son. In addition, Clarissa breaks her word to her brother, proclaims her love to Mentivole, the son of Baptista and friend to Cesario, and gives him her brother's ring.

At loose ends for entertainment, the two young men decide to hold a horse race which Cesario wins after he interferes with his friend's mount. Mentivole, believing his honor attacked, draws his sword and slightly wounds Cesario. This trivial cheating incident escalates into a full-blown vendetta between the two families. Troubles are then compounded for the Alberti with the news that the Admiral has been drowned at sea. Biancha, the Fair Maid of the title, is also introduced, together with other low denizens of the hostelry—Forobosco the conjurer, his attendant Clown, and assorted suitors (all probably created by Webster). Cesario now shows himself a proud, self-indulgent snob as he suggests to Biancha that he deserves some sexual recompense for bestowing his "uncommon favours" upon her. But Biancha's virtue and modesty prove successful against his advances.

Recalled to Florence, Cesario is astonished when his mother, Mariana, brings suit to disown him, claiming that he is of low birth. Her flimsy motivation, revealed to the audience but not to Cesario, is to protect him from the enmity of the Baptisti who are now perforce reconciled to him, since his new social status makes vengeance incompatible with honor. Accepting his lot, Cesario delivers an impassioned speech on virtue as the sign of true nobility, which so touches the Duke that he orders Mariana (his mother) to marry the young man so as to ennoble him. Hearing of Cesario's fall from high estate, the gentle Biancha now comes to offer him both her virtuous consolation and her love, since difference of rank is no longer an obstacle to their marriage.

But the ambitious Cesario heartlessly spurns her for bigger game:
"Unskild, what hansome toys are maids to play with! / How innocent!
but I have other thoughts / Of nobler meditation—my felicity"
(4.1.143–45). He refuses Mariana's frantic solution that they marry in
name only and instead proposes a match with Clarissa, reminding her
of their close (yet chaste) affection. Mariana falls into a frenzy at this
possible incest, offers Cesario all her property, and curses Clarissa if she
even thinks of the match. The girl, however, says that her love is
already given to Mentivole, who reciprocates it. Thus Cesario is left
lamenting (rather offhandedly) that he has lost all three women: "I can
but dye a Batchelor, thats the worst on't" (4.1.306).

The peripheral activities of Forobosco and the denizens of the inn
now prefigure the abundant revelations and reconciliations of the final
act. Webster even dares to gull both the stage characters and the
audience simultaneously, as he forces his Clown to perform in a diabolical
dance. The play then concludes with an explosion of information. Alberto
has survived shipwreck, fortuitously rescued from the galleys by Prospero.
The vendetta between the Alberti and the Baptisti is revived, with the
fathers threatening single combat and the lovers planning suicide.

Then Prospero, along with Juliana, Baptista's wife (who has spent
the last twelve years in a monastery), and Biancha, arrive to act as
composite deus ex machina. Friendship is restored, and the Fair Maid
is revealed as the daughter of Baptista and the well-born Juliana. The
nobility of Biancha's blood has triumphed; nature has been proved
superior to nurture. She is now a fitting match in rank for Cesario. A
new era of unity begins with a double wedding about to take place,
while the rogue Forobosco and his Clown are sent to the galleys.

Critical comments.   This is a patchwork play, not of the first
rank, and more preposterous in terms of situation and motivation than
A Cure for a Cuckold. Like its predecessor, it takes its title from the
subplot, and uses the same theme of love-honor-friendship. The contrivance by which a mother legally disowns her son at the expense of
her own honor repeats *The Devil's Law-Case,* with equally dubious
motivation. A dramatic device from *Anything for a Quiet Life* also
reappears in the skillful gulling of the audience by the deliberate
withholding of evidence. Once again there is a multilevel plot, divided
between upper and lower classes, but unlike *A Cure for a Cuckold* there
is a moral constant in the charming figure of Biancha, the Fair Maid,
whose virtue is unassailable and whose breeding is finally revealed to

be as noble as her virtue. Critics customarily consider her worthy of a better play and certainly of a better hero.

At the beginning Cesario is a somewhat pompous and hypocritical young man, as he instructs his sister in the virtue he does not propose to practice himself. Later, his relationship with Clarissa is one of barely repressed incest. In friendship he is likewise undependable and Mentivole quite rightly prefers not to compete with him because he is a bad loser. Caught cheating, his defense is rage. He is also devious in carrying out Alberto's sentence on Mentivole. With hairsplitting reminiscent of *A Cure for a Cuckold,* he decides to take his friend's sword rather than amputate the hand that wields it. At first this decision to defy his father's orders seems laudable, but a second thought forces the realization that Cesario has still insulted Mentivole's honor by confiscating its outward token of courtly chivalry.

In his treatment of the charming Biancha he is both exploitive and heartless. Certainly, he extols her virtue to his sister, Clarissa, but that is merely to prove the superior strength of his commitment to family honor. Her snobbery toward Biancha prefigures his own when he attempts to cajole the Fair Maid from virtue, and consequently his courtroom peroration on the superiority of nature over nurture, on virtue as the true nobility, appears insincere. His ambition in spurning the virtuous charms and fidelity of Biancha for Clarissa, to say nothing of his incestuous desires, reveals him to be a shallow young man indeed, a mother's boy of a courtier to whom quarreling and self-gratification are a way of life. In other words, he is unworthy of Biancha, who again becomes attractive to him only when he is jilted by another, and discovers her to be of birth superior, not merely equal, to his own: "*Biancha* daughter to a princesse!" (5.3.264). He deserves neither her love nor her forgiveness. But by the convention of tragicomedy, they are married.

Clarissa and Mentivole, the other young couple, are romantic stereotypes, lovers of exceptional fidelity, despite a series of apparently unsurmountable obstacles. Both they and Baptista offer echoes of *Romeo and Juliet* and of Shakespeare's romances with their happy endings. Clarissa's fidelity redeems, in part, her initial snobbery toward Biancha.

Except for Biancha, the characters are cardboard figures, manipulated by the events of the play rather than acting from carefully conceived motivations. Though perhaps not entirely Webster's creation, Biancha remains a delightful figure, memorable in her simplicity, recalling his *Fayre and happy Milke-mayd* of the Overburian characters and also reminiscent of the Flower Maidens of Shakespeare's romances. Although like them she is also virtue personified, Biancha is vaguely unsatisfactory because she does not exert their reforming, uplifting moral suasion. She possesses charm in abundance, but initially it strikes no permanently responsive chord in her lover and arouses nothing more than passive admiration from other characters.

Shakespeare's *Tempest* comes to mind with the coincidentally named revelatory figure of Prospero. But this play is no *Tempest* and he is no magician; that role is assigned to Forobosco, a faking, blustering conjurer, the liveliest figure of the play, and probably an authentic Webster creation. He springs with such life from the printed page that one is tempted to allow him considerable importance and see the quarrel between Forobosco and his Clown as a commentary on the unpredictable battles among the nobles. Then with regret one must acknowledge that his role is so peripheral that it could easily be excised, with no one the wiser except the specialist in Webster.

The entire action is a proliferation of confusions, a collection of coincidences, and a flurry of reconciliations arising from contrivances worthy of a fairy tale. Nonetheless, it is possible to imagine this play as an effective stage piece, with duels fought or threatened, a courtroom scene, barely averted incest, the reunion of a lost family, and clandestine lovers.

The Fair Maid of the Inn is a good journeyman piece, the kind of play that one reads with some interest to discover the seventeenth-century equivalent of a modest Broadway or West End success. Webster's hand is hard to detect, and there is nothing that exhibits the dark brilliance of some aspects of his earlier tragicomedy, *The Devil's Law-Case*. Even the exploitation of the incest motif, with its attendant horror-taboo, is a pale recollection of *The Duchess of Malfi*. But there are echoes, and the play has sufficient charm and dramatic interest to repay analysis.

Appius and Virginia

Date, text, sources, and authorship. The date of this play is disputed with scholars placing it both at the beginning and at the end of Webster's career. An early date is postulated on alleged parallels between *The Rape of Lucrece* (1608) by Thomas Heywood, Webster's collaborator, while similar echoes of Shakespeare's *Julius Caesar* (1599) and *Coriolanus* (1608) have also been cited. However, these two plays were not printed before the First Folio of 1623. Arguments for a later date include the extremely effective courtroom scene of *Appius and Virginia* which offers a mature treatment comparable with *The Devil's Law-Case* rather than *The White Devil*. Corroborating negative evidence also comes from its omission from the dedication to *The Devil's Law-Case* (1623), unless it is one of the "others"—plays whose titles are not given.

Topical references seem to support a late date. The famine in the Roman camp and the refusal of the Senate to send food to its troops, original to the play, may refer to an incident in the Low Countries in 1624–25 when an English expeditionary force lost two-thirds of its complement of 12,000 to starvation. However, the action of Virginius in nearly bankrupting himself to help his men, mirrors the reaction of decent officers to the parsimony of Queen Elizabeth to her impressed navy and army. An image drawn from "the inflammability of flax" (5.1.163–66) has been traced to a London disaster of 1623,[14] while a joke about a soldier's stomach striking twelve was also used by Heywood in his *English Traveller,* acted around 1627, and published in 1633.

Contemporary scholarship now tentatively proposes this play as Webster's last work, written in collaboration with Heywood, after *A Cure for a Cuckold* and *The Fair Maid of the Inn.* This offers the symmetrical and acceptable thesis that in his last play Webster returned to the successful tragic mode of his maturity, old-fashioned though some critics may think it. It also suggests 1627 as the earliest possible date for this play while the latest is unsure, because of our ignorance of the exact date of Webster's death. Verification seems unlikely and definitive evidence can do no more than place *Appius and Virginia* somewhere in the last period of his dramatic career.

Stage history also offers very little help, since details of the play's first performance are lost. It has been identified with the last play on a list dated 10 August 1639 of dramatic properties assigned for sole performance to "The King and Queen's young company of players at the Cockpit [also known as the Phoenix] in Drury Lane," under the direction of William Beeston.[15] In 1691 Gerard Langbaine asserted that *Appius and Virginia* had been well received in his day. This comment may refer to an adaptation by Thomas Betterton for performance at the Duke's Theatre, "an old play" which Samuel Pepys saw in 1669 under the title of *The Roman Virgin, or the Unjust Judge.*[16]

The circumstances of its publication in 1654 are equally obscure, and once again, in the absence of any provenance for the text, one cannot know either the nature of the original manuscript copy or the extent of alterations in the playhouse and printing shop. The title page reads as follows:

APPIUS / AND / VIRGINIA. / A / TRAGEDY. / BY / *JOHN WEB-STER*. / [Printer's Device] / *LONDON*, / Printed for *Rich. Marriot*, in S. *Dunstans* / Church-Yard *Fleet-street*. 1654.

The text was reprinted in 1655, 1659, and again in 1679, with a notation of Betterton's performance on the title page.

The ascription of sole authorship to Webster has no supporting evidence beyond his name on the title page of the First Quarto. No one thought to question the matter until Rupert Brooke in 1913 argued that the entire play was by Thomas Heywood. Brooke caused other scholars to look more closely at the text, examining linguistic habits, then employing metrical tests, and more recently, studies of imagery. The general consensus now is that Webster probably plotted the course of the play, wrote the major part of it, and may even have revised some of the scenes written by Heywood who, except for 3.2, was responsible for the character of the bawdy clown Corbulus.[17]

The chief source of the play is the account of Dionysius of Harlicarnassus in his *Roman Antiquitities* (book eleven), possibly supplemented by reference to Livy, the master of annalistic Roman history (book 3). Dionysius had been translated into English by Philemon Holland (1600), which Webster, with his customary dependence on translations, probably used. But all that is sure is that some major details of the play are found only in Dionysius, most notably the ruse by which Appius pretends unwillingness to undertake the responsibility of rule. Similarly, some important arguments of the trial scene come from there, but Webster also exercises a considerable amount of compositional freedom in his use of material, notably in those additions which may have some topical significance.[18]

Synopsis. Appius Claudius, a duplicitous patrician, is elected one of the *Decemviri* after masking his ambition with apparent reluctance. More evidence of his wickedness comes when he enlists the help of the underhanded plebeian Marcus Clodius in obtaining "The rich fee-simple of *Virginia's* heart" (1.3.43). Clodius suggests that Appius withhold from her father, Virginius the noble Roman commander, the money that should be appropriated for the payment of his troops. In this way he can blackmail Virginia into accepting his demands. If this plan proves unsuccessful, then Appius can use his other weapons of "feare and power" (1.3.60).

In the meantime, Virginius has ridden posthaste to Rome to plead before the Senate for his men, who lack even food and military supplies. Enraged at the Senators' parsimonious treatment of the city's defenders, he so insults the Senators that his request is refused. He then swears he will bankrupt himself rather than see his men starve. Before he returns to his camp he meets with Virginia and arranges her betrothal to Icilius. Appearing before his mutinous troops, Virginius regains their loyalty to Rome by saying that the funds he is about to distribute come from Appius and the Senate, not himself.

Back in Rome, Icilius petitions Appius to send money to Virginius because his personal payments to the army threaten the future of Virginia's dowry. Appius, thinking to exploit what looks like greedy self-interest, promptly offers to provide Icilius with a better match, but the young man recognizes the ruse as an act confirming Virginia's allegations of the patrician's lust. He draws his dagger with the threat, "I'l nail thee to the Chair" (2.3.104), but when Appius denies involvement with Virginia he decides to bide his time.

Clodius, now secretary to Appius, has devised a new solution for his superior. He will arrange to have Virginia declared a slave so that she can become Appius's strumpet; he has no need to marry her now. To that end he arranges the arrest of Virginia, claiming that the girl has been passing herself off as noble, but that in fact she is his lowborn slave. Clodius now brings suit before Appius, demanding the return of his "slave," Virginia, and calls for immediate trial. Icilius wishes to delay the trial until the return of Virginius, and Appius, to avert suspicion, agrees. However, he sends orders that Virginius be detained in the camp.

His plan does not work, and Virginius reaches Rome in time for the full trial before the tribunal of Appius. Once again Webster has developed a superb courtroom scene, comparable to his earlier one in *The Devil's Law-Case.* On that occasion there was a "spruce lawyer," Contilupo; now a "spruce," or crooked Orator, pleads the case for Clodius. Both Virginius and Virginia appear dressed in the garb of slaves to gain the sympathy of the court, but they are out-argued since the warrior Virginius is unskilled in the manipulative verbal weapons of the law. The honest words of Numitorius, a possible beneficiary of the suit, go unheeded, as the Orator calls for immediate sentence.

Pandemonium breaks out, with all the defendants pointing to flaws in the evidence. Just as Appius starts to pronounce sentence, Virginius begs leave to bid farewell to his daughter, and in lyrical words of fatherly tenderness he recalls his joy in her childhood and his now dashed hopes for her. Then, as soon as Appius awards her to Clodius, Virginius draws his dagger, kills his daughter to free her from the lust of the corrupt judge, and rides off to the starving camp.

Arriving bloodstained and half-crazed, he tells his tale, with the result that the entire army places itself under his command and marches to Rome to exact justice upon Appius. The Senate now sends representatives to parley with Virginius, but there is dissension in Virginius's family, with Icilius berating him as "a noble *Roman,* / But an unnatural Father" (5.1.110–11) who has destroyed his hopes for happiness. However, they are reconciled and the young man exhorts Virginius to use his military power wisely.

Appius and Clodius are now imprisoned, each blaming the other for his defeat. With the arrival of Virginius, Icilius, and other Romans bearing Virginia's bleeding body, a new, semi-official, trial scene ensues in which Appius begs for mercy, appealing to Virginius's sense of honor in returning mildness for cruelty and thereby establishing his own greatness. As the noble Virginius vacillates, Icilius fears that he will again place Appius in the chair of justice.

But the army, by carrying the body of Virginia in procession through the streets, has incited a rebellion against the *Decemviri*. Mercy is now dead in the heart of Virginius, but he still offers both criminals a chance to die with honor, handing each a sword so that they can die "in the high Roman fashion." Appius accepts the offer and kills himself, but the plebeian Clodius refuses and is remanded to the common hangman. Blood will out, and the lowborn man dies as a criminal, while Appius at least dies with honor. The tyrannous authority of the *Decemviri* is no more, and Virginius and Icilius become consuls (historically they were tribunes). As one might expect from the author of a Lucrece play, Heywood, to whom the final scene belongs, praises Virginia and her precursor both for their devotion to chastity and their role in bringing about the rebirth of Roman liberty.

Critical comments.   Corruption in justice and politics, love and lust, and the relationship between woman victims and political advancement are constant tragic themes in the work of John Webster

from the early collaborative *Sir Thomas Wyatt* to *Appius and Virginia*.[19]
Even the criminally guilty Vittoria in *The White Devil* is to some extent
the feminine victim of an ambitious family, while the chastely sensual
heroine of *The Duchess of Malfi* is certainly that. This theme is muddied
in the rather antifeminist *The Devil's Law-Case* by the strongly manipulative figure of Leonora, but the victimization of Angiolella and,
to a lesser extent, Jolenta prevents its entire disappearance.

Thus it is in character for Webster to make use of the popular
combination of feminine chastity, rape, and politics in this, probably
his final play. Further, the choice of the tale of Virginia is also predictable,
if one considers the identity of his collaborator, Thomas Heywood,
already the author of *The Rape of Lucrece* (1608), for the lives of both
victim-ladies had been considered mirrors of each other since Roman
times. But both stories are romantic history. Indeed, modern classical
scholarship doubts Livy's accuracy in recounting the tyranny of Appius,
suggesting that the connection with Virginia was a poetical legend
probably based on the suicide of Lucrece some sixty years earlier rather
than a political exemplum. However, since both deaths were followed
by a rebellion, the conflation of chaste victim with the lust of a tyrant
is made sequential, indicating that private lust is emblematic of public
evil. Thus the guilty men are removed from office and their victims
are glorified as sacrifices to the cause of liberty and examples of chastity
for all women to emulate. Yet today their status as sacrificial offerings
to a curiously limited masculine interpretation of honor detracts from
wholehearted feminist praise since, in the case of *Appius and Virginia,*
filicide is apparently a justifiable response.

Heywood contributes further to this moral confusion by allowing
Appius to die nobly as a Roman, by his own hand, thereby salvaging
his honor as a patrician, while the miserable plebeian Clodius cannot
muster the courage for such an act. The very fact that Virginius wavers
in his attitude toward Appius, even seriously thinking of showing him
mercy, may indicate either the father's remorse for filicide or a complicated
legalistic attitude toward the *decemvir's* guilt. The crime of Appius was
planned, but not committed, and hence he can be punished only for
his intention. At the same time it also demonstrates greater respect for
the Roman code of honor than love for the slaughtered girl. But though
dying with dignity as a suicide, Appius still cannot be said to possess
the "integrity of life" that Webster's earlier characters celebrate. Again,
the moral center of this Webster play is confused.[20]

Further conflicting attitudes come from the clown, Corbulus, most of whose bawdy humor is also written by Heywood.[21] The Clown and the Nurse are basically stereotypical and irrelevant to the plot, but they do have importance for the theme: their colloquies act as counterpoint to the unassailable but threatened virtue of Virginia.

This typical use of contrast is also demonstrated in the character of Clodius. He is much more important in the play than in the sources, and from his first appearance to his death he serves a contrapuntal purpose. He is a shrewd plotter, a resourceful planner of evil, the one who devises the easiest means for Appius to possess Virginia. He has a flexible and facile intellect, reacting with skill and speed to his master's improvisations, notably in the abortive trial scene of 3.2 when Appius suddenly turns against him. There are also hints of skillful planning in 4.1, where the entire exchange among Appius, Clodius, and the Orator seems a "practis'd Dialogue" (4.1.142). In the same way the virtuous and valiant Virginius, continually led by his emotions, contrasts with the outwardly disciplined Appius, whose external control masks inner turmoil. Similarly, Numitorius and Icilius, with their shrewdness and rationality, represent another contrast.

The climactic scene of this play is the trial (4.1), but the scene in the prison (5.2), a simulated trial, is almost as significant. In the preliminaries to the lawsuit Appius is shown cleverly defanging the opposition, seeming to support them by upbraiding and threatening to imprison his co-conspirator. But in the main confrontation, Webster returns to his earlier strengths as a dramatist with his legal satiric barbs well sharpened. The virtuous Virginius, defeated by the legalisms of corruption, is driven by despair to the direct action of the warrior. But once again disjunction rules in his lyrical (some might say sentimental) farewell to the unsuspecting Virginia, when verbal tenderness is transmuted into unexpected violence and stated with the sexual echoes of the fate of Thyestes' children (4.1.346–47).

The shock value of this scene notwithstanding, the final section also demonstrates a cardinal difficulty with *Appius and Virginia*. The characters are drawn from the outside so that their motivations are not fully developed. Virginius's murderous reaction is unexpected, because nothing is fully revealed about his inner, emotional life. The trial scene allows him his expression of love, yet it lacks credibility because it comes from a poetically undeveloped character. Without revelatory soliloquies as a guide, one cannot know what lies beneath the appearance and must regard the play with detachment. The reader remains aloof from the action, admiring, evaluating and sifting it, but not becoming deeply involved with it. *Appius and Virginia* then, is somewhat chilly. If admirable in its use of rhetoric, careful in its linear construction, classical in its discipline, noble in its assertion of ideals, yet it still lacks "heart." It is a worthy conclusion to Webster's dramatic career but it lacks the earlier despairing splendor of those memorable characters who make and meet their destruction with transcendent human dignity.

Spurious Plays

Two plays formerly attributed to Webster are no longer accepted as his: *The Weakest Goeth to the Wall*, published anonymously in 1600; and *The Thracian Wonder* (1661), attributed by the publisher, the ubiquitous Kirkman, to Webster and Rowley. The first of these was assigned to Webster as late as 1675, but it bears no resemblance to his work and there is no external evidence to connect him with it. *The Thracian Wonder*, however, sported a title page that almost duplicated that of *A Cure for a Cuckold* and came from the same untrustworthy publisher. But again, there appears to be no merit in the ascription.

The last attribution that needs to be dispensed with is Webster's alleged additions to *The Spanish Tragedy*, the famous revenge play by Thomas Kyd. These are mentioned in Henslowe's diary in 1602, recording payments of around £5 to Ben Jonson for them, an extraordinarily large amount for a mere 340 lines. Their only attachment to Webster is their treatment of death and madness, but that was already the theme of the original play. In addition, as Lucas points out, they do not sound like the work of the John Webster who at that time was laboriously writing *Sir Thomas Wyatt*.[22]

Conclusion

Scholarship on Webster is currently in the ascendant: each year dissertations, articles, and books proliferate. But it was not always thus. Webster was barely remembered when Charles Lamb, in his *Specimens of the English Dramatic Poets, Who Lived about the Time of Shakespeare* (1808) compared him favorably with Shakespeare and reprinted scenes from *The White Devil, The Duchess of Malfi, The Devil's Law-Case,* and *Appius and Virginia.* Moreover, Webster's work held the stage throughout the nineteenth century only by dint of considerable adaptation, and because actresses enjoyed playing the passionate roles of his two great tragic heroines. Webster was generally considered to be a poet who happened to write drama, as Swinburne perceived him in the 1880s. Webster's two great tragedies were admired, and their funerary laments suitably anthologized, while that redoubtable group of Victorian literary scholars who founded the original Shakespeare Association included him, sometimes disparagingly, in their researches into the nature of non-Shakespearean drama.

The twentieth century concentrated first on authorship studies, and much valuable work was done in an attempt to identify Webster's part in his numerous collaborations. Such works as *Anything for a Quiet Life, A Cure for a Cuckold,* and *The Fair Maid of the Inn* then found their way into the canon. Other spurious plays followed, like *The Thracian Wonder* and *The Weakest Goeth to the Wall,* only to be excluded later. The numerous essays of H. Dugdale Sykes are responsible for much of this material, but authorial studies have always been a cottage industry with Webster. Even today the early works, of E. E. Stoll (1905) and F. E. Pierce (1909) remain useful despite their heavy reliance on subjective judgment and the sole test of parallel passage. But critical studies were not neglected, and Rupert Brooke's 1911–12 Oxford master's thesis remains of interest despite its youthful exuberance and sometimes questionable judgments.

Text and sources have been well treated by modern scholars, with the F. L. Lucas edition (4 vols., 1927–28) an excellent and successful example of solid scholarship combined with a true missionary desire to reawaken interest in Webster. Though some later editions of the independent plays have superseded Lucas, his comprehensive work remains the standard one. Sources have been exhaustively treated by Robert W. Dent (1960) who gives a definitive listing of the voluminous borrowing perpetrated by the playwright. Later scholars have built upon Dent's foundation and are now paying attention to the poetic transmutation wrought upon sometimes commonplace materials. For the independent tragedies, Gunnar Boklund has produced two extraordinarily detailed volumes (1947, 1962) identifying all the known source material appropriated by Webster. In addition, Webster himself has finally been identified by Mary Edmond (1976, 1980) so that formerly obscure references can now be explained. Then, with the publication of the work of Fernand Lagarde (1968) and Charles Forker (1986), Webster has finally received his long-awaited encyclopaedic treatment.

Certain themes have always predominated in Webster studies, most particularly the nature of his moral vision. Some scholars have pondered the apparent lack of conventional religious beliefs and attitudes, while others have upheld his commitment to the established religion. His ambivalence always attracts critics, who frequently see it as an extraordinary objectivity in portraying "this busy trade of life." It is this constantly shifting viewpoint, this evenhanded neutrality in the portrayal of both good and evil, that shows a questing mind at work, while his unique sense of the macabre and his preoccupation with the tomb continually remind us of "the common bellman" who recalls not only the Newgate criminal but all humanity to their last end.

Analysis of Webster's dramatic structure is a topic of considerable comment. Here the work of Inga-Stina (Ekeblad) Ewbank, particularly in her influential and frequently anthologized essay, "The 'Impure' Art of John Webster" (1958), is especially noteworthy. She identifies the "disjunctive" quality of his work, his deliberate undercutting, and his ability to keep his audience on the *qui vive* with his constantly shifting ironic and sometimes grotesquely unexpected perspective. The trial and death of Vittoria, together with the resurrection of Flamineo in *The White Devil,* and the discovery scene, passion, and death of the Duchess of Malfi are superb examples of the way in which Webster can control the emotions and reactions of his audience by presenting opposed points of view, mixed tones, and questions left forever unanswered.

Character studies have also been an important element in Webster studies; in this regard his treatment of women is paramount. Vittoria of *The White Devil* and the heroine of *The Duchess of Malfi* have always attracted attention because of their strength of character, whether in villainy or virtue. Today, critical attention also includes Leonora of

The Devil's Law-Case as another strong woman, and with the increase in feminist scholarship the emphasis on Webster as portrayer of dominant female figures has developed significantly. But despite their challenge to the *mores* of their day, Webster's tragic women retain their conventional role as victims, while the tragicomic Leonora succeeds in remarriage to a younger man. The morality of their behavior is also a common topic of debate, particularly in considerations of the Duchess of Malfi and her possible contribution to her own guilt. Is she, like Vittoria, the White Devil, to be considered guilty, or is she innocent, or a combination of both? What, precisely, did Webster intend?

Interest in Webster's thoroughly fascinating villains has also continued, with Bosola, the Machiavel with a heart, a popular subject, along with that astonishing collection of wicked brothers who are the source of evil in the three independent plays. Exploitive villainy in the character of Flamineo in *The White Devil* shades into incestuous passion finally made public in Ferdinand's confession in *The Duchess of Malfi,* while the Cardinal of the same play doubles as hostile brother and the wicked churchman of the preceding play. Romelio, the "fortunate young man" of *The Devil's Law-Case,* is a skillful development of these other brothers in his manipulative treatment of his sister and general amorality. Modern psychology is now frequently employed in the attempt to explain such characters, and their actions with a concomitant development in the depth of stage portrayal. At the same time, however, one must be wary of imposing a full psychiatric examination of them because they also contain many conventional elements.

Amorality may well be a key to an understanding of Webster's world where corruption in all kinds of human relationships is endemic, and even love is destroyed by the power of evil. The gates of hell indeed seem to prevail, but the ineffective virtue of Cornelia in *The White Devil* and the steadfast love of the Duchess demand our respect. Curiously, so too does the superb defiance of Vittoria.

Webster's settings also epitomize this theme of quotidian evil, popularly assumed to be pervasive in Italy, the home of "that Godless Renaissance below the Alps," as Roger Ascham put it. If for Ascham "an Italianate Englishman is a devil incarnate," for Webster, with typical English propagandistic chauvinism, an Italian was apparently all hell let loose, particularly if he was also a churchman. Even the remorsefully pregnant Angiolella in *The Devil's Law-Case* epitomizes something of the easy virtue of representatives of Roman Catholicism in Webster's astonishing gallery of morally ambivalent characters. But if one accepts the definition of evil in Thomas Aquinas as an "absence of good," one can evaluate the playwright's attention to the perverse as a moral statement that evokes comment on and enforces commitment to its virtuous obverse.

Today Webster's place in the history of English drama is more secure than ever, and professional performance is beginning to reflect this fact. Like Shakespeare in *Troilus and Cressida* and the problem plays, which have achieved their current status and critical relevance only in the twentieth century, Webster speaks with the authority of moral urgency over four hundred years of history to a kindred century which continually echoes Jacobean skepticism as it espouses relativism yet laments the decline of values and the demise of the old primary certitudes. For Webster was a questioner of establishment values and more than any other playwright of his time he did indeed give the devil his due.

Perhaps these are some of the reasons for the burgeoning interest in this strange dramatic phenomenon who rose mysteriously and briefly from the anonymous mists of collaboration to flourish with a unique voice in two tragedies and an underrated tragicomedy. He then submerged himself again in collaborations, surfacing only as the author of a Lord Mayor's Procession and perhaps a last tragedy, *Appius and Virginia,* before slipping unnoticed into the ultimate and universal nullity of the grave. But this was a preoccupation that he had pursued with intensity throughout his career.

Appendix

Verses ascribed to John Webster on the unique 1633 edition of a 1625 engraving of King James and his family, living and dead, used as the frontispiece to this book. Contractions have been expanded. Reproduced by kind permission of the British Library.

Catalogue: BL 1849-3-15-15

G

Hev propere nimis coronandae
Haec cum parca duo dulcia pignora regis
flebilis agnouit crimen et erebuit
When Fate before their due matured tyme
Pulld these two branches from their royal stem
The Fates themselues confest their heedles crime
and in acknowledgment did blush for shame.

F

Diis Genita; & magnos progeniture Deos
Happy Coniunction which to men doth show,
So blest an Influence, such blisse below;
The same as when in their high sphears aboue
The God of War do meet and Queene of Loue.

B

Mors sceptra hegionibus aequat.
Queene Ann resignes her Scepter vnto fate,
and yet in death you may obserue her State
which outshines all the Iewels of the Crowne,
shee left behind her, a most deare renowne:

A

Tu decus omne tuis
Ars vtinam mores animumque essingere posset
pulchrior in terris nulla Tabella soret.
Could Art his guiftes of mind express as well.
no Picture in the World should this excell.

C

Vno Auulsumon deficit Alter.
Prince Henry (to our generall sorrow) died
eure his beloued Sister was a bride;
Never did a great Spright earlier shoot
but the Prime blossomes seldome become fruict

D

Virescit vulnere virtus
Great in thy birth, & greater in thy choice,
but absolutly greatest in the voice
proclaimes thee constant, vnder fortun's spight
thus envy, death and hell thou putst to flight

E

Phaenix
Vnica semper auis
One Phoenix at a Tyme, and this is shee:
sweet as her funerall nest of Spicery
o may your father, from your fruictful wombe.
plant vniversall peace in christendome.
                    Haec composuit—Ioannes Webster

Notes and References

In these notes the following frequently mentioned works of scholarship are given short citations: M. C. Bradbrook, *John Webster: Citizen and Dramatist* (New York: Columbia University Press, 1980); Robert W. Dent, *John Webster's Borrowing* (Berkeley and Los Angeles: University of California Press, 1960); Mary Edmond, "In Search of John Webster," *Times Literary Supplement* (24 December 1976):1621–22, and also *Times Literary Supplement* (11 March 1977):272 and (24 October 1980):1201; Charles Forker, *Skull Beneath the Skin: The Achievement of John Webster* (Carbondale and Edwardsville: Southern Illinois University Press, 1986); F. L. Lucas, ed., *The Complete Works of John Webster,* 4 vols. (London: Chatto & Windus, 1927–28).

Chapter One

1. Edmond, *TLS* (24 December 1976):1621–22. Later corroborative information was contributed by Mark Eccles in a letter, *TLS* (21 January 1977):71. Edmond added further material in two more letters, *TLS* (11 March 1977):272 and (24 October 1980):1201. See also the opening chapter of Forker. For a cautious summary of the facts known prior to 1976 see F. L. Lucas, ed., *The Duchess of Malfi* (New York: Macmillan, 1959), 9–12, a revision of his earlier researches; cf. Lucas, ed., *Works,* 1:49–56. Unless otherwise stated, all citations and quotations are from this edition. Bradbrook, 10–46, and elsewhere, gives a broadly based and sometimes circumstantial account of the playwright's life.

2. Edmond, *TLS* (24 December 1976):1622.

3. The date of 1579/80 also makes sense when considered in reference to a mention of Webster as one of several playwright-collaborators in 1602.

4. Forker, 22, reproduces the text of the prayer to be said on that occasion.

5. Edmond, *TLS* (24 December 1976):1621–22. See also Forker, 21–25.

6. See Bradbrook, 20–27, and Forker, 30–39, for comments on the curriculum and supposed fellow students of Webster at the school.

7. Edmond, *TLS* (24 December 1976):1621.

8. Ibid.

9. Lucas, ed., *Works,* 1:50. The Inns of Court still exist and form the center of legal life in the city of London. They also play an important role in the training of barristers in England. Under that legal system there

is a distinction between trial lawyers, who plead cases, and solicitors, who prepare the briefs. The barrister operates on a taxi-rank system, accepting clients offered him and pleading a case solely on the basis of law and the facts presented to him. Charles Laughton in the well-known film *Witness for the Prosecution* is a barrister; so is *Rumpole of Old Bailey*. In the United States this distinction is not formally observed, although to some extent it exists in practice.

10. Lucas, ed., *Works,* 1:50; Forker, 41.

11. Edmond, *TLS* (24 October 1980):1201.

12. Forker, 5. See also Edmond, *TLS* (24 December 1976):1622, nn. 42, 60.

13. Edmond, *TLS* (24 December 1976):1622, suggests "shortly before February 26, 1614/15."

14. Forker, 8. Of course, since he had not served an apprenticeship he could only become a member by right of primogeniture after the death of his father.

15. For an early and shrewd guess see R. G. Howarth, "John Webster," *Times Literary Supplement* (2 November 1933):751.

16. *Certain Elegies done by Sundrie Excellent Wits* (London, 1618), sigs. F6v–7.

17. Preface to *The White Devil,* ed. Lucas, *Works,* 1:107.

18. Peter B. Murray, *A Study of John Webster* (The Hague: Mouton, 1969), 20. For a discussion of the fine line between *imitatio* and plagiarism see Stephen Orgel, "The Renaissance Artist as Plagiarist," *English Literary History* 48 (1981):476–95.

19. The most comprehensive identification of Webster's appropriation of the work of others is that of Robert W. Dent. For source materials of individual works see the relevant chapters.

20. William Heminges, *Elegy on Randolph's Finger* (London, 1632). See Edmond, *TLS* (24 December 1976):1621.

21. Edmond, *TLS* (24 December 1976):1622.

Chapter Two

1. Forker, 65–66.

2. Lucas, ed., *Works,* 4:239.

3. Lucas, ed., *Works,* 4:241. For detailed treatment of Webster's probable contribution see: F. E. Pierce, *The Collaboration of Webster and Dekker,* Yale Studies in English, no. 31 (New York: Henry Holt, 1909), 132–59. E. E. Stoll (*John Webster* [1905; reprint, New York: Gordian Press, 1967], 49–54) allows very little to Webster. Lucas (ed., *Works,* 4:239–41) is also conservative. Fredson Bowers, in his four-volume edition, *The Works of Thomas Dekker* (Cambridge: Cambridge University Press, 1953–61), 1:399–404, gives a very precise account of the textual difficulties but does

not concern himself with authorship. For this material see Cyrus H. Hoy, "Introduction, Notes, and Commentaries to Texts," in Bowers, ed., *The Works of Thomas Dekker,* 4 vols. (Cambridge: Cambridge University Press, 1980), 3:312–14. Unless otherwise stated, all citations and quotations from the Dekker collaborations are from this edition.

4. Supporters of the Earl of Essex paid the Lord Chamberlain's Men 40 shillings to perform *Richard II* the day before the rebellion took place, perhaps hoping that it might aid in inciting support. The players, however, were exonerated of subversive intent. For the contemporary significance of *Sir Thomas Wyatt* see Judith Doolin Spikes, "The Jacobean History Play and the Myth of the Elect Nation," *Renaissance Drama,* n.s., 8 (1977):117–49.

5. Forker, 124.

6. Lucas (ed., *Works,* 3:296–98) thinks it futile to speculate about any other contributions to the total play; M. L. Wine (ed., introduction to *The Malcontent,* Regents Renaissance Drama Series (Lincoln: University of Nebraska Press, 1964), xiii) agrees, saying that any attempt to identify Webster's contribution beyond that of the *Induction* is "a thankless task."

7. G. K. Hunter, introduction to John Marston, *The Malcontent,* The Revels Plays (London: Methuen, 1975), xlvi–liii. Unless otherwise stated, all citations and quotations from *The Malcontent* are from this edition. Hereafter cited in the text. For contrary opinions see Stoll, 55–62; Forker, 74; David J. Lake, "Webster's Additions to *The Malcontent:* Linguistic Evidence," *Notes & Queries,* n.s., 28 (April 1981):153–58.

8. Wine, ed., xxiv–xxv.

9. Forker, 76; Bradbrook, 114–17.

10. Jacqueline Pearson, *Tragedy and Tragicomedy in the Plays of John Webster* (Totowa, N. J.: Barnes & Noble, 1980), 46–49.

11. Forker, 76.

12. For discussion of the contributions of each author to these two plays see Pierce, 29–132; Stoll, 62–82; Lucas, *Works,* 4:239–44; Peter B. Murray, *A Study of John Webster* (The Hague: Mouton, 1969), 23–30, appendix 2, 264.

13. Bowers, ed., *Works,* 2:313–17.

14. Bowers, ed., *Works,* 2:407–9.

15. Lucas, ed., *Works,* 4:241, 243; Stoll, 62–82.

16. The *Oxford English Dictionary* notes this play as the source for the first printed appearance of the term "Westward for smelts" (2.3.81) to describe this situation.

17. Personal examination of this artifact at the Victoria and Albert Museum, London, suggests the near-necessity of promiscuity, even in a bed of such remarkable size.

18. Forker, 96–97, notes the deliberate parody of Chapman's play, *The Tragedy of Charles, Duke of Byron.*

19. Alexander Leggatt, *Citizen Comedy in the Age of Shakespeare* (Toronto: University of Toronto Press, 1973), 134.

20. Lucas, ed., *Works,* 4:239–44. See also Stoll, 62–79.

21. Murray, 28, and appendix 2, 264; see also Forker, 84, 101–3.

22. Forker, 99–102, notes numerous other foreshadowings of events, images, and themes of the later plays.

Chapter Three

1. John Webster, *The White Devil,* ed. John Russell Brown, The Revels Plays (Cambridge: Harvard University Press, 1960), 3–4. Unless otherwise stated, all quotations and citations from *The White Devil* are from this edition.

2. For a detailed analysis of the text see John Russell Brown, "The Printing of John Webster's Plays, I, II, and III," *Studies in Bibliography* 6 (1954):117–40; 8 (1956):113–27; 15 (1962):57–69.

3. Dent (57–59) believes that the play was for the most part written considerably earlier than its publication date, noting that only two definite sources were published after 1608.

4. For an excellent short stage history of *The White Devil* see Brown, ed., lviii–lxii. For a more comprehensive account see Forker, 453–90, passim.

5. Nahum Tate, *Injur'd Love: or The Cruel Husband* (London, 1707), 72. See Tso-Liang Wang, *The Literary Reputation of John Webster to 1830,* Jacobean Drama Studies, no. 59 (Salzburg: Institut für Englische Sprache und Literatur, Universität Salzburg, 1975), 49–62, for a detailed examination.

6. Forker, 488.

7. One of these children was Virginio Orsini, who visited England at the end of the sixteenth century as part of the Italian embassy.

8. Such was the canon law of western, Roman Catholic Europe until the Council of Trent (1547–63), from which England was specifically *excluded.* Under the canon law of the Church of England, however, such clandestine unions were made invalid by the *Constitutions and Canons Ecclesiastical* (1604). See Margaret Loftus Ranald, " 'As Marriage Binds, and Blood Breaks': English Marriage and Shakespeare," *Shakespeare Quarterly* 30 (1979):60–81. As the trained lawyer Webster probably was, he would know English, and perhaps Roman, canon law on this subject.

9. The historical Cardinal Montalto took the name of Sixtus V. He undertook considerable Vatican reforms and is remembered as a great builder of baroque Rome. He was responsible for placing the central obelisk in St. Peter's Square.

10. Gunnar Boklund, *The Sources of "The White Devil"* (Uppsala: Appelberg, 1957). See also Frederick O. Waage, *"The White Devil" Discover'd: Backgrounds and Foregrounds to Webster's Tragedy;* American University Studies, ser. 4, vol. 5 (New York: Peter Lang, 1984).

11. Boklund, 83.

12. See Dent, 67–173; Waage, *"The White Devil" Discover'd,* chapter 9, discusses at some length the thematic relationship between Webster's play and the Paul's Cross Sermon of Thomas Adams, *The Gallant's Burden,* and the *Biathanatos* of John Donne.

13. Dent, 69–70, suggests that the term could also be applicable to Brachiano.

14. Peter B. Murray (*A Study of John Webster* [The Hague: Mouton, 1969], 35n.) also makes this comparison. His chapter on *The White Devil* gives an interesting account of Elizabethan attitudes toward whiteness, particularly as it applies to women.

15. For an analysis of Vittoria's argumentative skill see H. Bruce Franklin, "The Trial Scene of Webster's *The White Devil* Examined in Terms of Renaissance Rhetoric," *Studies in English Literature: 1500–1900* 1 (1961):35–51.

16. See Robert Ornstein, *The Moral Vision of Jacobean Tragedy* (Madison: University of Wisconsin Press, 1960), 128–40, for a good analysis of this play.

17. Travis Bogard, *The Tragic Satire of John Webster* (Berkeley and Los Angeles: University of California Press, 1955), 38–44.

18. D. C. Gunby, in *Webster: "The White Devil,"* Studies in English Literature, no. 45 (London: Edwin Arnold, 1971), considers that evil is vanquished with the ascent of Giovanni to the Dukedom.

19. See Bogard, 17–19.

Chapter Four

1. This is a shortened version of a quotation from Horace that roughly translates as follows: "If you know precepts wiser than these of mine, please tell me; if you do not, then join me in their performance."

2. Webster, John, *The Duchess of Malfi,* ed. John Russell Brown, The Revels Plays (Cambridge: Harvard University Press, 1964), lx–lxviii. Unless otherwise stated, all citations and quotations from *The Duchess of Malfi* are from this edition. See also John Russell Brown, "The Printing of John Webster's Plays, I, II, and III," *Studies in Bibliography* 6 (1954):117–40; 8 (1956):113–27; 15 (1962):57–69.

3. Brown, ed., xvii.

4. Lucas, ed., *Works* 2:3. It is also possible that the Overbury volume had been circulating in manuscript prior to its printing date of 1614.

5. Brown, ed., xvii. See also J. Russell Brown, "On the Dating of Webster's *The White Devil* and *The Duchess of Malfi,*" *Philological Quarterly* 31 (1952):353–62.

6. For an excellent short stage history see Brown, ed., lv–lix. See also Don D. Moore, *John Webster and His Critics 1617–1964* (Baton Rouge:

Louisiana University Press, 1966), 151–60. For a more comprehensive account see Forker, 453–90, passim. Forker also gives an indispensable analysis of this play, 113–20, 296–369.

7. Both Lowin and Burbage had also played in *The Malcontent* and the *Induction* by Webster.

8. Brown, ed., xxiii, notes its intimate quality and numerous silences. For an account of performance difficulties see Robert Bruce Graves, "*The Duchess of Malfi* at the Globe and the Blackfriars," *Renaissance Drama,* n.s., 9 (1978):193–209.

9. Lucas, ed., *Works,* 2:4–5.

10. Theobald was the first editor to apply his knowledge of Elizabethan handwriting to the text and made the famous emendation in the Hostess's account of the death of Sir John Falstaff in *Henry V,* "and a'babbled of green fields" (2:3:16). Alexander Pope unjustly pilloried his work.

11. See Clifford Leech, *John Webster: A Critical Study* (London: Hogarth Press, 1951), 19–24, and Tso-Liang Wang, *The Literary Reputation of John Webster to 1830,* Jacobean Drama Studies, no. 59 (Salzburg: Institut für Englische Sprache und Literatur, Universität Salzburg, 1975), 62–78, for accounts of this play. Theobald's critical comments on Webster's work are more important than his adaptation as indicating the opinion of an early Elizabethan scholar.

12. Leech, *John Webster,* 19–25; see also Brown, ed., *The Duchess of Malfi,* lvi–lvii. See Frank W. Wadsworth, "Webster, Horne, and Mrs. Stowe: American Performances of *The Duchess of Malfi,*" *Theatre Survey* 11 (1971):151–66; and " 'Shorn and Abated'—British Performances of *The Duchess of Malfi,*" *Theatre Survey* 10 (1969):89–104, analyzing the changes made by Horne.

13. For an account of the contribution of Bertolt Brecht to this production and his own adaptation of the text see Milly S. Barranger, "The Shape of Brecht's *Duchess of Malfi,*" *Comparative Drama* 12, 1 (1978–79):61–74.

14. Forker, 488. He also notes adaptations into a novel by Davis Stacton, *Dancer in Darkness* (1960), and a television play by Kingsley Amis, set in the Caribbean, *A Question of Hell,* 1964.

15. Lucas (ed. *Works,* 2:11) notes that Bandello used the pseudonym Delio when he wrote his sonnets. In the notes to pp. 10–13 he also lists corroborative testimony from official Italian sources and changes made by Belleforest and William Painter from the original Bandello novella. For an extensive treatment of all the sources and versions of this tale see Gunnar Boklund, "*The Duchess of Malfi*": *Sources, Themes, Characters* (Cambridge, Mass.: Harvard University Press, 1962).

16. See Dent, 174–265.

17. Boklund, 54. See also Brown, ed., xxvii–xlii.

18. See Chapter 3 n.8; also Frank W. Wadsworth, "Webster's *Duchess of Malfi* in the Light of Some Contemporary Ideas on Marriage and Remarriage," *Philological Quarterly* 35 (1956):394–407.

19. This echoes the fate of Isabella in *The White Devil.*

20. Bradbrook, 154.

21. Lewis Theobald, *The Fatal Secret* (London, 1735), sig. A4v.

22. Bradbrook, 162.

23. Bradbrook, 164.

24. Inga-Stina Ekeblad, "The 'Impure' Art of John Webster," *Review of English Studies* 9 (1958):253–67. She notes that this ritual was sufficiently familiar in the nineteenth century for Thomas Hardy to put it in his novel *The Mayor of Casterbridge* as the Skimmington-ride. Natalie Zemon Davis has also suggested that *Hamlet* belongs to the charivari tradition. See also Frank W. Wadsworth, " 'Rough Music' in *The Duchess of Malfi:* Webster's Dance of Madmen and the Charivari Tradition," in *Rite, Drama, Festival, Spectacle: Rehearsals Toward a Theory of Cultural Performance,* ed. John J. MacAloon (Philadelphia: Institute for the Study of Human Issues, 1984), 58–75.

25. Robert Ornstein, in his excellent section on *The Duchess of Malfi* in *The Moral Vision of Jacobean Tragedy* (Madison: University of Wisconsin Press, 1960), 140–50, warns against interpreting this play in a "pietistic" manner. Clifford Leech (*Webster: "The Duchess of Malfi."* Studies in English Literature, no. 8 [London: Edward Arnold, 1963], 35–40) suggests that to some extent the Duchess is responsible for her fate, but William Empson ("Mine Eyes Dazzle," *Essays in Criticism* 14 [1964]:80–86) strongly disagrees.

26. Ornstein (*Moral Vision,* 141) suggests that Webster is concerned with the way his characters suffer the consequences of their choice rather than their motivations.

27. See most particularly Elizabeth M. Brennan, "The Relationship Between Brother and Sister in the Plays of John Webster," *Modern Language Review* 58 (1963):488–94.

28. Ellen Rothenberg Belton ("The Function of Antonio in *The Duchess of Malfi,*" *Texas Studies in Literature and Language* 18 [1976]:474–85) maintains that he represents the Christian ideal of endurance throughout the play.

29. See Forker, 134, and also 135–37, for a putative account of the contents of this play.

Chapter Five

1. See Gunnar Boklund, "*The Devil's Law-Case*—an End or a Beginning?", in *John Webster,* ed. Brian Morris (London: Ernest Benn, 1970), 113–30.

2. For a thorough analysis of this complex play see Forker, 138–44 and 370–450. For an account of Webster's use of sources see Dent, 289–315.

3. "With life, as with a play, it matters, not how long, but how good the performance." Lucas, ed., *Works,* 2:321.

4. Frances A. Shirley, ed., John Webster, *The Devil's Law Case,* Regents Renaissance Drama Series (Lincoln: University of Nebraska Press, 1972), xxiii. Unless otherwise stated, all citations and quotations from *The Devil's Law-Case* are from this edition.

5. See John Russell Brown, "The Printing of John Webster's Plays, I, II, and III," *Studies in Bibliography* 6 (1954):117–40; 8 (1956):113–27; 15 (1962):57–69.

6. Shirley, ed., 4; see also Forker, 142–43.

7. John Webster, preface to *The White Devil,* in Lucas, ed., *Works,* 1:107.

8. E. E. Stoll, *John Webster* (1905; reprint New York: Gordian Press, 1967), 31; Lucas, ed., *Works,* 2:214–16.

9. For a detailed account of this controversy see chapters 4 and 12 of Linda Woodbridge, *Women and the English Renaissance: Literature and the Nature of Womankind, 1540–1620* (Urbana: University of Illinois Press, 1984).

10. Forker, 138.

11. Lucas, ed., *Works,* 2:217.

12. Elizabeth M. Brennan, ed., *The Devil's Law Case,* New Mermaids (London: Ernest Benn, 1975), xi–xii; Dent, 308–9; Lucas, ed., *Works,* 2:217–21.

13. Bradbrook, 169–72; Forker, 138.

14. Forker, 385–87.

15. See Forker, 141–42. One is also reminded of Webster's two Overburian Characters, *A vertuous Widdow* and *An ordinarie Widdow,* in which a faithful mourning celibate relict is contrasted with a lusty remarrying woman—to the dispraise of the latter.

16. Again, a connection between this play and the Overburian characters by Webster can be found in *A Puny-clarke, A meere Petifogger,* and *A Reverend Judge.* See also Forker, 402.

17. For a good survey of resemblances see Forker, 374–79.

18. Ralph Berry (*The Art of John Webster* [Oxford: Clarendon Press, 1982], 165–67) has some good comments on Webster and the law in this regard.

19. John Fletcher, "To the Reader," *The Faithful Shepherdess,* ed. Cyrus H. Hoy. In Francis Beaumont and John Fletcher, *The Dramatic Works in the Beaumont and Fletcher Canon,* gen. ed., Fredson Bowers. Cambridge: Cambridge University Press, 1966–85, 3:(1976) 497.

20. Berry, *The Art of John Webster,* 167.

21. Jacqueline Pearson, *Tragedy and Comedy in the Plays of John Webster* (Totowa, N. J.: Barnes & Noble, 1980), 102–3.

22. Pearson, *Tragedy and Comedy,* 99; see also pp. 99–104; cf. Forker, 429–35.

23. For a representative survey see Peter B. Murray, *A Study of John Webster* (The Hague: Mouton, 1969), 214, chapter 11—185–214; D. C. Gunby, introduction to *The Devil's Law-Case*, in *John Webster: Three Plays* (Harmondsworth: Penguin Books, 1972); Berry, *The Art of John Webster*, 167; Madeleine Doran, *Endeavors of Art: A Study of Form in Elizabethan and Jacobean Drama* (Madison: University of Wisconsin Press, 1954), 354; Ian Scott-Kilvert, *John Webster*, Writers and Their Work, no. 175 (London: Longmans, Green, for the British Council, 1964), 39; Lee Bliss, *The World's Perspective: John Webster and the Jacobean Drama* (New Brunswick, N. J.: Rutgers University Press, 1983), 171–88.

24. Forker, 445, 450.

25. See Don D. Moore, *Webster: The Critical Heritage* (London: Routledge & Kegan Paul, 1981), for a series of illustrative quotations.

26. Doran, 139.

Chapter Six

1. Lucas, ed., *Works*, 3:259.

2. The text of this ode is reprinted in Lucas, ed., *Works*, 3:259–60. See also Forker, 102–3.

3. Lucas, ed., *Works*, 3:265. Text appears 3:260–61.

4. Lucas, ed., *Works*, 3:265.

5. For an account of the illness and death of Prince Henry see J. W. Williamson, *The Myth of the Conqueror: Prince Henry Stuart, a Study of 17th Century Personality* (New York: AMS Press, 1978), 149–70. He suggests the possibility that symptoms may have been present as early as the preceding June–July (152). See also Roy Strong. *Henry, Prince of Wales and England's Lost Renaissance*. New York: Thames and Hudson, 1986.

6. When Henry Bolingbroke, Duke of Lancaster, deposed Richard II in 1399, he had a teenage son, later Henry V. William the Conqueror, who became the first king of England after defeating an Anglo-Saxon confederacy, also had a living male heir.

7. Williamson (*Myth of the Conqueror*, 168) offers as possible murderers Robert Carr, Viscount Rochester, Frances Howard, Countess of Essex, Henry Howard, Earl of Northampton, and even King James.

8. Forker (110) suggests that this may be the source for the waxen effigies in *The Duchess of Malfi*; so does Lucas (ed., *Works*, 2:179–80) and David M. Bergeron ("The Wax Figures in *The Duchess of Malfi*," *Studies in English Literature, 1500–1900* 18 [1978]:331–39).

9. Lucas, ed., *Works*, 3:268. Prince Henry had been an honorary member of the Merchant Taylors', a circumstance that helps explain Webster's participation in the elegiac volume. Together with his parents, the Prince

had been feasted by the Company in 1607 (for which John Webster, Sr., was reimbursed 7s.6d.), and in 1610 sent them "Two brace of fatt bucks" from his own deerpark, an indication that membership in the guild may have been important to him (Forker, 26).

10. The term "night-peece" in the dedication recalls the dying line of Lodovico in *The White Devil*.

11. Dent, 266–78; Lucas, ed., *Works*, 3:285–90.

12. For the text of the poem see Lucas, ed., *Works*, 3:275–83. Hereafter cited in the text.

13. For the last line see *The Duchess of Malfi* (1:1:209), itself a borrowing from an earlier source. Dent, 270; Forker, 113.

14. Williamson, *Myth of the Conquerer*, 182.

15. In a further parallel, Edward, the Black Prince, also died before he could ascend the throne, though at a later age than Prince Henry, leaving a son who became the deposed Richard II.

16. Lucas (ed., *Works*, 3:287) calls lines 84–86 "surely the most detestable lines in Webster."

17. Dent (278) suggests this is derived from William Alexander, Earl of Stirling, *Croesus*, or perhaps a proverbial utterance.

18. Robert B. Bennett ("John Webster's Strange Dedication: An Inquiry into Literary Patronage and Jacobean Court Intrigue," *English Literary Renaissance* 7 [1977]:352–67) argues that Webster's dedication of *A Monumental Column* was meant sarcastically and satirically. Otherwise it seems singularly unfitting for a poem memorializing a prince supposedly free of Carr's defects.

19. See Lucas, ed., *Works*, 4:6–10, for notes on authorship. For analysis of and commentary on these characters see Forker, 120–34; Bradbrook, 167–69.

20. For a list of parallels to be found within the plays see Lucas, ed., *Works*, 4:10–14; for examination of source materials see Dent, 279–88.

21. Lucas, ed., *Works*, 4:26. Hereafter cited in the text.

22. It may be significant that Dent finds no source for either of these characters. They may come from Webster's own observation.

23. This is another character for which Dent lists no sources; again, it is one that smacks of personal observation.

24. Lucas (ed., *Works*, 4:57–58) notes that some of the arguments in this character come from Thomas Nashe, *Pierce Penniless, His Supplication to the Devil* (1592).

25. For an excellent essay on this character see Forker, 129–34.

26. The Webster family was, however, intimately connected with these earlier entertainments. John Webster, Sr., supplied "horses and charrett" at a cost of 30 shillings to transport scholars of the Merchant Taylors' School to the 1602 procession; in 1605, he was reimbursed 8s.6d. for expenses incurred at the building of the pageant; in 1613 he sued Thomas Dekker

to recover a debt of £40 for the hire of coaches for the pageant of 1612. See Edmond, *TLS* (24 December 1976):1261–62.

27. Forker, 164. It is highly possible that the playwright's brother, Edward Webster, provided pageant wagons for this Merchant Taylors' celebration. Paula Johnson ("Jacobean Ephemera and the Immortal Word," *Renaissance Drama*, n.s., 24 [1977]:151–71) gives a useful analysis of *Monuments of Honor*, noting Webster's attention to spectacle and expense and his "iconological exegesis" of the various displays, linking the ephemeral visual elements to immortal concepts.

28. This is the ceremony "derived from Antiquity" that Webster mentions. See Forker, 164–69, for an account of the entire proceedings. For other accounts see R. T. D. Sayle, *Lord Mayors' Pageants of the Merchant Taylors' Company in the 15th, 16th & 17th Centuries* (London: Eastern Press, 1938), 108, and David M. Bergeron, *English Civic Pageants: 1558–1642* (Columbia: University of South Carolina Press, 1971).

29. Lucas, ed., *Works*, 3:317, 1. 23. Hereafter cited in the text.

30. He is buried in the Duomo of Florence and a fresco by Paolo Uccello still marks the site, on the Gospel side of the church toward the Great Door.

31. It may be significant that Webster, who wrote so many dramatic roles for independent women, takes care to single out the feminine members of his guild.

32. On this occasion the discharging of 140 chambers cost the company £33.6s.8d. (Lucas, ed., *Works*, 3:330, n. 38).

33. For additional comments on this pageant see Bradbrook, 180–81.

34. Wagner, Bernard M., "New Verses by John Webster," *Modern Language Notes* 46 (1931):403–5. See Appendix for transcription.

Chapter Seven

1. Lucas, ed., *Works*, 4:66.

2. For discussion of authorship see H. Dugdale Sykes, "A Webster-Middleton Play: *Anything for a Quiet Life*," *Notes & Queries* 141 (1921):181–83; 202–4; 225–26; 300. For minority opinions see G. E. Bentley, *The Jacobean and Caroline Stage* (Oxford: Clarendon Press, 1941–68), 4:859–61, and Peter B. Murray, *A Study of John Webster* (The Hague: Mouton, 1969), 261–63. For a very detailed affirmative discussion see Fernand Lagarde, *John Webster* (Toulouse: Association des Publications de la Faculté des Lettres et Sciences Humaines, 1968), 1:179–87. Forker (145–46) gives an excellent short summary of the evidence for Webster's part, and on page 549, note 1, offers judicious comments on the work of other scholars. See also Dent, 60–61, for comments on borrowing. Lucas (ed., *Works*, 4:66–68) gives a detailed survey of Websterian parallels.

3. Forker, 146 and 549, nn. 8, 10.

4. Edmond, *TLS* (24 December 1976):1622; Forker, 160–64; C. J. Sisson, *Lost Plays of Shakespeare* (Cambridge: Cambridge University Press, 1936), 80–124.

5. "It has been proved" (Lucas, ed., *Works,* 3:29).

6. Forker, 171–73, notes that the theaters were closed because of the plague from mid-May to late September of 1625, a situation that further narrows the date of composition.

7. For other comments on source materials see Rupert Brooke, *John Webster and Elizabethan Drama* (New York: John Lane, 1916). appendix J, 260–75; Lucas, ed., *Works,* 3:5–9.

8. See Henry David Gray, "*A Cure for a Cuckold* by Heywood, Rowley and Webster," *Modern Language Review* 22 (1927):389–97; Lucas, ed., *Works,* 3:10–18; and Murray, 215–16 and appendix 3, 265–68. E. E. Stoll (*John Webster* [1905; reprint New York: Gordian Press, 1967], 33–43) accepts Kirkman's assignment of authorship to Webster and Rowley; Forker (171) is skeptical about Heywood's share, considering that if it exists, it is "minor," and Murray agrees.

9. His opening speech (2.1.1–22) is clearly in the tradition of the prose character, particularly that of *A Younger Brother* later immortalized in the *Micro-Cosmographie* of John Earle (1628). Lucas (ed., *Works,* 3:101) also notes this similarity.

10. Jacqueline Pearson (*Tragedy and Tragicomedy in the Plays of John Webster* [Totowa, N. J.: Barnes & Noble, 1980], 116–32) notes the verbal comedic emphasis of the play, examining its repetition of words and the proliferation of riddles and paradoxes, as does Forker, 175–81.

11. An indication of the differing approaches to this play can be seen in Forker, 172–89, and Murray, 215–36. Forker laments the lack of moral center in the play, while Murray notes its educational value, as well as its farcical qualities.

12. See Murray, 216–17. Edmund Gosse in 1883 suggested that the main plot would be better treated separately, and S. E. Spring-Rice did so in *Love's Graduate* (Oxford: H. Daniel, 1885), an action approved by Brooke, in *John Webster and the Elizabethan Drama,* 274–75, on "artistic" grounds. An earlier adaptation by Joseph Harris (*The City Bride: or, The Merry Cuckold* [London: 1696]), a professional actor, emphasized the Compass plot, omitting some of the bawdry, and including songs and dances to fit the taste of the time. The text is currently available in the Augustan Reprint Society Publication No. 36; introduction by Vinton A. Dearing (Los Angeles: William Andrews Clark Memorial Library, University of California, 1952). See also Tso-Liang Wang, *The Literary Reputation of John Webster to 1830,* Jacobean Drama Studies, no. 59 (Salzburg: Institut für Englische Sprache und Literatur, Universität Salzburg, 1975), 43–49.

13. Murray (263) says that the evidence for Webster's part in it "is even slighter than that for *Anything for a Quiet Life*"; Pearson (55) allows

it a "perhaps"; Bradbrook ignores it entirely; and Lucas assigns nine scenes, including all of the Forobosco plot, to Webster, but both he and H. Dugdale Sykes depend entirely on the untrustworthy criterion of verbal parallels, which, of course, can be argued both ways. Nonetheless, some of them are highly convincing and strike the reader with the thrill of recognition. Basing his finding on linguistic analysis, Cyrus H. Hoy ("The Shares of Fletcher and His Collaborators in the Beaumont and Fletcher Canon (V)," *Studies in Bibliography* 13 [1960]:100–8) suggests even more Websterian material: act 2, about half of act 4, and the major part of act 5. Forker (190), after conducting his own linguistic tests, corroborates the data adduced by Hoy, although he is equivocal about admitting the play into the Webster canon.

14. Lucas, ed., *Works,* 3:125–26; Forker, 201.

15. Lucas, ed., *Works,* 3:121, quoting Edmond Malone, *Shakespeare* (1821). See also Forker, 223.

16. Clifford Leech, *John Webster: A Critical Study;* Hogarth Lectures on Literature (London: Hogarth Press, 1951), 14–15. See also Forker, 223–24, who notes that Betterton "played Virginius to his wife's Virginia."

17. Brooke, *John Webster and the Elizabethan Drama,* appendix A, 165–210. This text is an expanded version of Brooke's 1913 article in *Modern Language Review.* See also Arthur M. Clark, "The Authorship of Appius and Virginia," *Modern Language Review* 16 (1921):1–17; H. Dugdale Sykes, *Sidelights on Elizabethan Drama* (Oxford: Oxford University Press, 1924), 108–39; H. D. Gray, "*Appius and Virginia:* by Webster and Heywood," *Studies in Philology* 24 (1927):275–89; and Lucas, ed., *Works,* 3:134–45. For a good summary see Peter B. Murray, *A Study of John Webster* (The Hague: Mouton, 1969), 237–38 and 269–70, and Forker, 202. For image studies see Inga-Stina Ekeblad, "Storm Imagery in *Appius and Virginia,*" *Notes and Queries* 201 (1956):5–7; Melvin Seiden, "Two Notes on Webster's *Appius and Virginia,*" *Philological Quarterly* 35 (1956):408–17.

18. Webster does not appear to have consulted Painter or the other English accounts in Geoffrey Chaucer, John Gower, or the crude earlier *Appius and Virginia* by R. B. (1575), in working on this play. Dent (59–63) also suggests as sources *The Diall of Princes* of Antonio de Guevara (1557) and *The Lord Coke his Speech and Charge* (1607).

19. Good critical analyses of *Appius and Virginia* are in Murray, 216–52, and Forker, 200–24.

20. See the corroborating comments of Murray, 250–52.

21. The clown of 3.3, however, recalls the Webster of the Overburian characters in his attacks on the lust and enterprise of recent widows.

22. See Stoll, *John Webster,* 34–37; Brooke, *John Webster and the Elizabethan Drama,* 212–13; Lucas, ed., *Works,* 4:241, 245–47.

Selected Bibliography

PRIMARY SOURCES

Independent Works

The Devil's Law-Case: or When Women Go to Law the Devil Is Full of Business. A New Tragicomedy. London, 1623. Probable date of composition, 1610–20.

The Tragedy of the Duchess of Malfi. London, 1623. Probable date of composition, 1612–13.

The White Devil, or, the Tragedy of Paulo Giordano Ursini, Duke of Brachiano, with the Life and Death of Vittoria Corombona the Famous Venetian Curtizan. London, 1612. Probable date of composition, 1610–12.

Collaborations

Appius and Virginia. London, 1654. With Thomas Heywood. Date of composition is disputed, divided between the beginning and end of Webster's career.

The Famous History of Sir Thomas Wyatt. With the Coronation of Queen Mary, and the Coming in of King Philip. London, 1607. With Thomas Dekker, Thomas Heywood, Wentworth Smith, and Henry Chettle. Webster's contribution is unknown, and the untrustworthy text seems to be a conflation of the two parts of *Lady Jane* (lost). Probable date of composition, 1602.

Induction to *The Malcontent*, by John Marston. London, 1604. Webster may also have supplied the subplot.

Northward Ho!. London, 1607. With Thomas Dekker.

Westward Ho!. London, 1607. With Thomas Dekker.

Conjectural Works

Anything for a Quiet Life. London, 1662. With Thomas Middleton. Probable date of composition, 1621–22.

A Cure for a Cuckold. London, 1661. With William Rowley. Probable date of composition, 1624–25.

The Fair Maid of the Inn. London, 1647. With Philip Massinger, John Ford, and William Rowley. Originally listed as by John Fletcher and included in the Beaumont and Fletcher Folio. Probable date of composition, 1625–26.

Lost and Spurious Plays

Caesar's Fall. With Thomas Dekker, Michael Drayton, Thomas Middleton and Anthony Munday. Mentioned in Henslowe's *Diary,* 1602. Lost. Probably the same as *Two Shapes.*

Christmas Comes but Once a Year. With Henry Chettle and Thomas Dekker. Mentioned in Henslowe's *Diary,* 1602. Lost. Probably a seasonal pot-boiler.

The Guise. Acted 1614–15. Lost.

A Late Murther of the Son upon the Mother, or Keep the Widow Waking. With Thomas Dekker, John Ford, and William Rowley. Acted 1624. Lost. An exploitation of two sensational crimes.

The Spanish Tragedy, with additions. London, 1602. The additions to the play by Thomas Kyd have been assigned to Webster on very slight, and now discredited, evidence.

The Thracian Wonder. London 1661. Allegedly by John Webster and William Rowley. Now considered spurious.

The Weakest Goeth to the Wall. London, 1600. Now considered spurious.

Nondramatic Works

Additional Characters in Thomas Overbury, *Characters.* Sixth Issue. London: 1615. Includes thirty-two new characters now assigned to Webster, who also edited the text.

Celebratory Ode in *Arches of Triumph,* by Stephen Harrison. London, 1604. An account of the formal triumphal entry of King James I into London.

Dedicatory Verses to *The Palmerin of England,* part III, by Anthony Munday. London, 1602.

Dedicatory Verses to *Apology for Actors,* by Thomas Heywood. London, 1612.

Dedicatory Verses to *The English Dictionarie . . .,* by Henry Cockeram. London, 1623.

A Monumental Column. London, 1613. Webster contributed one of the three memorial poems to the recently deceased Henry, Prince of Wales. The others were written by Cyril Tourneur and Thomas Heywood.

Monuments of Honor. London, 1624. Possibly Webster's last work, this is the text of the elaborate spectacle for the installation of John Gore, Merchant Taylor, as Lord Mayor of London.

Verses accompanying an engraving of King James I and his family living and dead, ca. 1624. Assigned to Webster. See frontispiece for reproduction of the 1633 issue and appendix for transcription of the text.

Editions

Dekker, Thomas. *The Dramatic Works of Thomas Dekker.* Ed. Fredson Bowers. 4 vols. Cambridge: Cambridge University Press, 1953–61. A well-edited text containing the best currently available source for *Westward Ho!* *Northward Ho!*, and *Sir Thomas Wyatt*.

Marston, John. *The Malcontent*. Ed. G. K. Hunter. The Revels Plays. London: Methuen, 1975. A reliable text with excellent introductory material.

———. *The Malcontent*. Ed. M. L. Wine. Regents Renaissance Drama Series. Lincoln: University of Nebraska Press, 1964. Good generally available text, with useful introduction.

Webster, John. *The Complete Works of John Webster*. Ed. F. L. Lucas. 4 vols. London: Chatto & Windus, 1927–28. Excellent scholarship, combined with an attempt to interest the general reader in Webster. In some cases later research has superseded this work, but except for the three independent plays, it remains the overall standard edition.

———. *The Devil's Law Case*. Ed. Elizabeth M. Brennan. New Mermaid Series. London: Ernest Benn, 1975. Good text and detailed introduction.

———. *The Devil's Law Case*. Ed. Frances A. Shirley. Regents Renaissance Drama Series. Lincoln: University of Nebraska Press, 1972. Good generally available text, with useful introduction.

———. *The Duchess of Malfi*. Ed. F. L. Lucas. New York: Macmillan, 1959. A revision of the 1927 edition.

———. *The Duchess of Malfi*. Ed. John Russell Brown. The Revels Plays. Cambridge: Harvard University Press, 1964. Good text with introduction strong on textual and stage history.

———. *John Webster: Three Plays*. Introduction by D. C. Gunby. Harmondsworth: Penguin Books, 1972. Generally available text of the three independently written plays. Good introduction calls for a revaluation of *The Devil's Law-Case*.

———. *The White Devil*. Ed. John Russell Brown. The Revels Plays. Cambridge: Harvard University Press, 1960. Good text with introduction strong on textual and stage history.

———. *The White Devil*. Ed. J. R. Mulryne. Regents Renaissance Drama Series. Lincoln: University of Nebraska Press, 1969. Good generally available text with useful introduction.

Adaptations

Barranger, Milly S. "The Shape of Brecht's *Duchess of Malfi*." *Comparative Drama* 12, 1(1978–79):61–74. Analysis of the adaptation by Bertolt Brecht (1933) in collaboration with W. H. Auden. Notes the added scenes, transpositions, and focus on Marxist theory.

Betterton, William. *The Roman Virgin: or The Unjust Judge*. 1669? An adaptation of *Appius and Virginia*. Not located.

Harris, Joseph. *The City Bride: or, The Merry Cuckold*. London: 1696. Augustan Reprint Society Publication no. 36. Introduction by Vinton A. Dearing. Los Angeles: William Andrews Clark Memorial Library,

University of California, 1952. Adaptation of *A Cure for a Cuckold*, drawn from the subplot of the play.

Horne, R. H. *"The Duchess of Malfi": Reconstructed for Stage Presentation.* London: Davidson, 1851. Adapts, regularizes, and reconstructs the adaptation performed in England and the United States throughout the nineteenth century, driving the original from the boards. See Wadsworth, below.

Spring-Rice, S. E. *Love's Graduate.* Oxford: H. Daniel, 1885. Adaptation of the main plot of *A Cure for a Cuckold.*

Tate, Nahum. *Injur'd Love: or The Cruel Husband.* London, 1707. Adaptation of *The White Devil* into pedestrian verse.

Theobald, Lewis. *The Fatal Secret.* London, 1735. Adaptation of *The Duchess of Malfi* with a happy ending. Has some interesting critical comments on the structure of the original play, which he unsuccessfully attempts to reduce to a more "classical" mode.

SECONDARY SOURCES

Bibliographies and Reference Materials

Carnegie, David. "A Preliminary Checklist of Professional Productions of the Plays of John Webster." *Research Opportunities in Renaissance Drama* 26 (1983):55–63. Productions of *The White Devil, The Duchess of Malfi, The Devil's Law-Case,* 1612–1983.

Corballis, Richard, and Harding, J. M., compilers. *A Concordance to the Works of John Webster.* Salzburg Studies in English Literature. Jacobean Drama Studies, no. 70. 3 vols. in 11 parts. Salzburg: Institut für Anglistik und Amerikanistik, Universität Salzburg, 1978–79. A computer-generated concordance to the canon, giving act, scene, and line citations for each reference.

Ewbank, Inga-Stina. "Webster, Tourneur, and Ford." In *English Drama (Excluding Shakespeare): Select Bibliographical Guides,* ed. Stanley Wells, pp. 113–33, London: Oxford University Press, 1975.

Howard, Tony. "Census of Renaissance Drama Productions." *Research Opportunities in Renaissance Drama* 23 (1980):55–71. Annotated entries with critical and evaluative comments.

Logan, Terence P., and Smith, Denzell S., eds. *The Popular School: A Survey and Bibliography of Recent Studies in English Renaissance Drama.* Lincoln: University of Nebraska Press, 1965. See the essay and bibliography by Don D. Moore, "John Webster," pp. 84–104, for a succinct rehearsal of facts and a good choice of selected annotated materials. The section entitled "William Rowley" contains discussion of the authorship of *A Cure for a Cuckold.*

Mahaney, William E. *John Webster: A Classified Bibliography.* Jacobean Studies, no. 10. Salzburg: Institut für Englische Sprache und Literatur, Universität Salzburg, 1973. Comprehensive and generally accurate. Includes references on stage history and historical milieu as well as criticism, editions, sources, dating, biography, literary history, and editions.

Moore, Don. D., compiler. "Recent Studies in Webster (1972–1980)." *English Literary Renaissance* 12(1982):369–75. Bibliography with annotation of major items.

Schuman, Samuel, compiler. *John Webster: A Reference Guide.* Boston: G. K. Hall, 1985. An annotated bibliography covering the period 1602–1981. Organized chronologically with a good index. Generally accurate.

———, compiler. "John Webster on Stage: A Selected Annotated Bibliography. In *Jacobean Miscellany,* no. 4, pp. 99–128. Salzburg: Institut für Anglistik and Amerikanistik, Universität Salzburg, 1985. Listing of theatrical productions with annotations.

Shapiro, Michael. "Annotated Bibliography on Original Staging in Elizabethan Plays." *Research Opportunities in Renaissance Drama* 23(1981):23–49. Copiously annotated list of works on English staging 1576–1642, many of which concern Webster.

Stagg, Louis Charles, compiler. *An Index to the Figurative Language of John Webster's Tragedies.* Charlottesville: Bibliographical Society of the University of Virginia, 1967. Excerpts "a key term from each image," presenting them in an alphabetical listing, and identifying the plays in which they appear.

———. *Index to the Figurative Language of the Tragedies of Shakespeare's Chief Seventeenth-Century Contemporaries: Chapman, Heywood, Jonson, Marston, Webster, Tourneur, and Middleton.* Ann Arbor: University Microfilms International for the Memphis State University Press, 1977. An expansion of the author's 1967 volume.

Criticism

Because of the numerous reference materials listed above, the following bibliography is highly selective, including major books, articles, and portions of books suitable for an introduction to the scholarship on the work of John Webster. See also *Notes and References.*

Barroll, J. Leeds, *et al. The Revels History of Drama in English.* Vol. 3. London: Methuen, 1975. Has some useful essays on Jacobean drama in general and a separate essay on Webster. See Kernan, Alvin.

Berggren, Paula S. "Womanish Mankind: Four Jacobean Heroines." *International Journal of Woman's Studies* 1 (1978): 439–62. Feminist study considering Vittoria and the Duchess as subverting masculine superiority.

Berry, Ralph. *The Art of John Webster*. Oxford: Clarendon Press, 1972. Based on the central thesis of law in opposition to evil. Uses analogies from art history to develop the idea that Webster is a "baroque" playwright, exemplified by his preoccupation with the grotesque, etc.

Bliss, Lee. *The World's Perspective: John Webster and the Jacobean Drama*. New Brunswick, N. J.: Rutgers University Press, 1983. Examines Webster as a conservative moralist and experimental dramatist whose art responds to contemporary concerns.

Bogard, Travis. *The Tragic Satire of John Webster*. Berkeley and Los Angeles: University of California Press, 1955. "Integrity of life" is a constant in the major characters of *The White Devil* and *The Duchess of Malfi*, where Webster "made the satiric voice coequal with the tragic."

Boklund, Gunnar. "*The Devil's Law-Case*—an End or a Beginning?" In *John Webster*, ed. Brian Morris, pp. 113–30. London: Ernest Benn, 1970. More original than the two great tragedies and influenced by Fletcher's work in tragicomedy, the play deals with topics other than nobility. It looks back at the tragedies and ahead to new ideas of drama.

———. "*The Duchess of Malfi*": *Sources, Themes, Characters*. Cambridge: Harvard University Press, 1962. A painstaking and exhaustive study of the playwright's sources.

———. *The Sources of "The White Devil."* Uppsala: Appelberg, 1957. A painstaking and exhaustive study of the playwright's sources.

Bradbrook, M. C. *John Webster: Citizen and Dramatist*. New York: Columbia University Press, 1980. Part 1 is a biography based on the work of Mary Edmond. Suggests that Webster was influenced by the careers of Lady Penelope Rich and Antonio Perez, the Spanish ambassador. Part 2 analyzes the dramas.

Brennan, Elizabeth M. " 'An Understanding Auditory': An Audience for John Webster." In *John Webster*, ed. Brian Morris, pp. 3–19. London: Ernest Benn, 1970.

———. "The Relationship Between Brother and Sister in the Plays of John Webster." *Modern Language Review* 58(1963):488–94. Examines the close and sometimes perverse relationships depicted.

Champion, Larry S. *Tragic Patterns in Jacobean and Caroline Drama*. Knoxville: University of Tennessee Press, 1977. Discusses self-interest as a ruling passion in *The White Devil*. *The Duchess of Malfi*, though portraying the same corrupt society, has a virtuous heroine who is destroyed by forces external to herself.

Courtade, Anthony Edward. *The Structure of Webster's Plays*. Jacobean Drama Series, no. 97. Salzburg: Institut für Anglistik und Amerikanistik, Universität Salzburg, 1980. Webster's use of Jacobean conventions in *The White Devil* (multiple focus), *The Duchess of Malfi* (punishment for violation of social mores), and *The Devil's Law-Case* (optimistic conclusion).

Dent, Robert W. *John Webster's Borrowing.* Berkeley and Los Angeles: University of California Press, 1960. The indispensable study of Webster's appropriation of the work of other writers, with emphasis on the three independent plays and *A Monumental Column.*

Dwyer, William W. *A Study of Webster's Use of Renaissance Natural and Moral Philosophy.* Jacobean Drama Studies, no. 18. Salzburg: Institut für Englische Sprache und Literatur, Universität Salzburg, 1972. Argues that Webster operates within the boundaries of established Christian ideals.

Ekeblad, Inga-Stina. "The 'Impure' Art of John Webster." *Review of English Studies* 9 (1958):253–67. An important study of Webster's disjunctive technique. Frequently reprinted in collections of critical essays.

———. "Webster's Constructional Rhythm." *English Literary History,* 24 (1957):165–76. Studies *A Cure for a Cuckold* to show how the scenic rhythm parallels that of other Webster plays, making this structural comparison a better guide than parallel passages to establishing authorship.

Ewbank, Inga-Stina. "Webster's Realism, or 'A Cunning Piece Wrought Perspective.'" In *John Webster,* ed. Brian Morris, pp. 157–78. London: Ernest Benn, 1970. Techniques of "reading" perspective pictures assist in interpreting *The White Devil* and *The Duchess of Malfi.*

Forker, Charles R. *Skull Beneath the Skin: The Achievement of John Webster.* Carbondale and Edwardsville: Southern Illinois University Press, 1986. An essential study of all aspects of Webster's work. Has an interesting section on "The Love-Death Nexus."

Goodwyn, Floyd Lowell, Jr. *Image Pattern and Moral Vision in John Webster.* Jacobean Studies, no. 71. Salzburg: Institut für Englische Sprache und Literatur, Universität Salzburg, 1977. Imagery as a reflection of morality in *The White Devil* and *The Duchess of Malfi.*

Gunby, D. C. "*The Devil's Law-Case:* An Interpretation." *Modern Language Review* 63 (1968):545–58. A didactic thesis play. Although Romelio is a villain-hero, guilty of pride, he is redeemed.

———. "*The Duchess of Malfi:* A Theological Approach." In *John Webster,* ed. Brian Morris, pp. 178–204. London: Ernest Benn, 1970. Webster is a didactic believer, not a despairing pessimist.

———. *Webster: "The White Devil."* Studies in English Literature, no. 45. London: Edward Arnold, 1971. Close critical reading of the play. Considers that evil is vanquished with the ascent of Giovanni to the dukedom.

Holdsworth, R. V., ed. *Webster, "The White Devil" and "The Duchess of Malfi": A Casebook.* London: Macmillan, 1975. Aimed primarily at an undergraduate audience, it presents a varied collection of material, biographical, critical and theatrical, as well as a good introductory essay.

Hoy, Cyrus H. "Critical and Aesthetic Problems of Collaboration in Renaissance Drama." *Research Opportunities in Renaissance Drama* 19 (1976):3–6. Discusses the history of and problems attendant upon attribution studies, particularly the Webster/Dekker collaborations.

———. "The Shares of Fletcher and His Collaborators in the Beaumont and Fletcher Canon (V)," *Studies in Bibliography* 13(1960):100–08. Discusses *The Fair Maid of the Inn.*

Hunter, G. K., and Hunter, S. K., eds. *John Webster: A Critical Anthology.* Baltimore: Penguin, 1969. Fifty-two items of previously published scholarship, some only in brief excerpts, covering contemporary criticism, later attempts to evaluate Webster, and modern opinions.

Jardine, Lisa. "*The Duchess of Malfi:* A Case Study in the Literary Representation of Women." In *Teaching the Text,* ed. Susanne Kappeler and Norman Bryson, pp. 203–17. London: Routledge, 1983. Discusses the Duchess of Malfi as a strong woman character and compares her with Vittoria in *The White Devil* and Beatrice-Joanna in Thomas Middleton and William Rowley's *The Changeling.*

Jenkins, Harold. "The Tragedy of Revenge in Shakespeare and Webster." *Shakespeare Survey* 14(1961):45–55. Examines Webster's adaptation of the revenge play genre to his own purposes. His protagonists suffer revenge rather than inflict it. Their reward is the grave.

Jump, John D. *"The White Devil" and "The Duchess of Malfi."* Notes on English Literature. Oxford: Basil Blackwell, 1966. Solid general and comparative study of both plays.

Kernan, Alvin. "The Plays of John Webster." In J. Leeds Barroll, *et al, The Revels History of Drama in English.* Vol. 3. London: Methuen, 1975. A most useful essay, ranking Webster very high. Sees him as believing in the existence of goodness and virtue in a corrupt world.

Kusoniki, Akiko. "A Study of *The Devil's Law-Case* with Special Reference to the Controversy over Women." *Shakespeare Studies* (Japan) 21 (1982–83):1–33. Relates the play to Jacobean antifeminism.

Lagarde, Fernand. *John Webster.* 2 vols. Toulouse: Association des Publications de la Faculté des Lettres et Sciences Humaines, 1968. A massive if hard-to-find text covering Webster's life, sources, texts, use of Machiavellian characters, place in Elizabethan and Jacobean theater, and reputation. Concludes with a history of criticism and theatrical productions. Particularly good treatment of feminine characters. In French.

Lake, David J. "Webster's Additions to *The Malcontent:* Linguistic Evidence." *Notes & Queries,* n.s., 28 (April 1981):153–56. Authorial study.

Leech, Clifford. "An Addendum to Webster's Duchess." *Philological Quarterly* 37 (1958):253–56. Argues against Frank W. Wadsworth; thinks the Duchess is at fault for marrying beneath her rank.

————. "Three Times *Ho* and a Brace of Widows: Some Plays for the Private Theater." In *The Elizabethan Theatre 3,* ed. David Galloway, Hamden, Conn.: Shoe String Press, 1973, pp. 14–33. A study of the cross-referential material in the three *Ho!* plays and their contemporary significance, particularly concerning the remarriage of widows.

————. *Webster: "The Duchess of Malfi."* Studies in English Literature, no. 8. London: Edward Arnold, 1963. Detailed analysis of construction and consideration of the probable reaction of a Jacobean audience. Discusses matrimonial law in this regard.

————. *John Webster: A Critical Study.* London: Hogarth Press, 1951. A succinct introduction with brief bibliography, stage history, and critical analysis of individual plays. Biographical details predate the research of Mary Edmond.

McDonald, Charles O. *The Rhetoric of Tragedy: Form in Stuart Drama.* Amherst: University of Massachusetts Press, 1966. A detailed study of *The White Devil,* discussing it as a representative of decadent Stuart drama.

McLeod, Susan H. *Dramatic Imagery in the Plays of John Webster.* Jacobean Studies, no. 68. Salzburg: Institut für Englische Sprache und Literatur, Universität Salzburg, 1977. Verbal and presentational images in *The White Devil* (reward and punishment), *The Duchess of Malfi* (appearance vs. reality, and disease), and *The Devil's Law-Case* (tragicomic reversals).

McLuskie, Kathleen. "Drama and Sexual Politics." In *Drama, Sex and Politics,* ed. James Redmond, pp. 77–91. Themes in Drama, no. 7. Cambridge: Cambridge University Press, 1985. Imagery, sexual politics, and the character of the Duchess of Malfi.

Moore, Don D. *John Webster and His Critics 1617–1964.* Baton Rouge: Louisiana University Press, 1966. A history of Webster criticism with some attention to stage history.

————. *Webster: The Critical Heritage.* The Critical Heritage Series. London: Routledge & Kegan Paul, 1981. A collection of excerpted comments presented chronologically, with a general introduction.

Morris, Brian, ed. *John Webster.* London: Ernest Benn, 1970. A valuable collection of ten new essays on the structural and philosophical issues in the plays, performance history, and other aspects of the work of John Webster. Includes items listed separately in this bibliography.

Mulryne, J. R. *"The White Devil* and *The Duchess of Malfi."* In *Jacobean Theatre,* Stratford-upon-Avon Studies, no. 1. Edited by Bernard Harris and John Russell Brown, pp. 200–25. London: Edward Arnold, 1960. Notes the language and setting of *The White Devil* and the mixed reactions evoked. *The Duchess of Malfi* has a consistent moral viewpoint.

————. "Webster and the Uses of Tragicomedy." In *John Webster,* ed. Brian Morris, pp. 131–55. London: Ernest Benn, 1970. Defines tragicomedy as a play in which neither genre is dominant, and discusses the mixture of styles and lack of moral absolutes in Webster.

Murray, Peter B. *A Study of John Webster.* The Hague: Mouton, 1969. A useful short study with separate chapters on the three independent plays. Webster is not so much a moralist as a tragic writer who perceives a higher order in the universe. Includes a section on authorship of the *Ho!* plays.

Ornstein, Robert. *The Moral Vision of Jacobean Tragedy.* Madison: University of Wisconsin Press, 1960. Chapter 5 is devoted to John Webster. Considers *The Duchess of Malfi* "a relatively detached study of the moral cowardice that robs life of meaning," and a more mature play than *The White Devil.*

Pearson, Jacqueline. *Tragedy and Comedy in the Plays of John Webster.* Totowa, N. J.: Barnes & Noble, 1980. The tragicomedies and Webster's experiments in "ordering extreme contrasts within a single dramatic structure."

Peterson, Joyce E. *Curs'd Example: "The Duchess of Malfi" and Commonwealth Tragedy.* Columbia: University of Missouri Press, 1978. Blames the Duchess for the tragedy because in marrying Antonio she fails as a ruler.

Pierce, Frederick Erastus. *The Collaboration of Webster and Dekker.* Yale Studies in English, no. 31. New York: Henry Holt, 1909. Attempts to distinguish the work of each dramatist using the test of parallel passages.

Rabkin, Norman, ed. *Twentieth Century Interpretations of "The Duchess of Malfi": A Collection of Critical Essays.* Englewood Cliffs, N. J.: Prentice-Hall, 1968. A valuable selection of previously published critical essays and excerpts. Includes some items listed separately in this bibliography.

Ribner, Irving. *Jacobean Tragedy: The Quest for Moral Order.* New York: Barnes & Noble, 1962. The tragedies of John Webster rise above his otherwise journeyman work. He portrays a corrupt world devoid of values and meaning where "Integrity of life" is the only constant.

Ridley, M. R. *Second Thoughts: More Studies in Literature.* London: Dent, 1965. Has an extensive section on *The White Devil* and *The Duchess of Malfi.*

Scott-Kilvert, Ian. *John Webster.* Writers and Their Work, no. 175. London: Longmans, Green, for the British Council, 1970. A short introductory survey. Webster inverts morality by gaining approval for amoral characters. Revision of 1964 edition.

Seiden, Melvin. *The Revenge Motif in Websterian Tragedy.* Jacobean Drama Studies, no. 15. Salzburg: Institut für Englische Sprache und Literatur, Universitität Salzburg, 1973. The tragedies of Webster are "punitive tragedies" unlike other Jacobean plays of the genre.

Smith, A. J. "The Power of *The White Devil.*" In *John Webster,* ed. Brian Morris, pp. 69–90. London: Ernest Benn, 1970. Discussion of the theatricality and deliberate incongruity of the play.

Spivack, Charlotte. "*The Duchess of Malfi:* A Fearful Madness." *Journal of Women's Studies in Literature* 1(1979):122–32. For the first time, women appear as heroic characters in English drama. Discusses the Duchess as an example of the complete woman who, though destroyed by men, exerts a salvific influence.

Sternlicht, Sanford. *John Webster's Imagery and the Webster Canon.* Jacobean Drama Studies, no. 1. Salzburg: Institut für Englische Sprache und Literatur, Universität Salzburg, 1972. Imagery and image clusters in *The White Devil, The Duchess of Malfi,* and *The Devil's Law-Case,* notably those of death, sex, war, and disease.

Stilling, Roger. *Love and Death in Renaissance Tragedy.* Baton Rouge: Louisiana State University Press, 1976. Has a section on *The White Devil* and *The Duchess of Malfi.* Notes Webster's almost feminist interest in strong women characters, and the problems faced by lovers in an inimical universe.

Stodder, Joseph Henry. *Moral Perspective in Webster's Major Tragedies.* Jacobean Drama Studies, no. 48. Salzburg: Institut für Englische Sprache und Literatur, Universität Salzburg, 1974. The conflict between good and evil is demonstrated in the conflict of characters, yet each one has some admixture of its opposite. However, in the end retributive justice rules.

Stoll, Elmer Edgar. *John Webster.* 1905. Reprinted New York: Gordian Press, 1967. Discusses dating and authorship of individual plays, particularly *A Cure for a Cuckold, The Thracian Wonder,* and *The Weakest Goeth to the Wall.* Divides Webster's career into three parts: Apprenticeship, Revenge Plays, and the Fletcherian and Eclectic Period.

Strong, Roy. *Henry, Prince of Wales, and England's Lost Renaissance.* New York: Thames and Hudson, 1986.

Thompson, Peter. "Webster and the Actor." In *John Webster,* ed. Brian Morris, pp. 21–44. London: Ernest Benn, 1970. Discusses modern problems in acting Webster.

Tomlinson, T. B. *A Study of Elizabethan and Jacobean Tragedy.* Cambridge: Cambridge University Press, 1964. Discusses *The White Devil* and *The Duchess of Malfi* at some length, considering the former a powerful play, yet a failure, and the latter an intellectual tour de force demonstrating how virtue can overcome moral chaos.

Waage, Frederick O. *"The White Devil" Discover'd: Backgrounds and Foregrounds to Webster's Tragedy.* American University Studies, ser. 4, vol. 5. New York: Peter Lang, 1984. Aims, through close reading of the text, "to assert the involvement of Webster in the literary and philosophical life of his time." Includes background essays.

Wang, Tso-Liang. *The Literary Reputation of John Webster to 1830.* Jacobean Drama Studies, no. 59. Salzburg: Institut für Englische Sprache und Literatur, Universität Salzburg, 1975. Includes an account of adaptations and performances.

Whigham, Frank. "Sexual and Social Mobility in *The Duchess of Malfi.*" *PMLA* 100 (1985):167–86. An anthropological study of the topic. Includes comments on incest.

Index